The Race

Hope,
Thank you
for being part
of our journey!
We love you!
Lori

THE RACE

A STORY OF GOD'S TIMING AND GRACE AND FINDING JOY IN THE JOURNEY

Lori Grant

Heavenly
Light Press
Alpharetta, GA

The author has tried to recreate events, locations, and conversations from her memories of them. The author has made every effort to give credit to the source of any images, quotes, or other material contained within and obtain permissions when feasible.

ISBN: 978-1-63183-459-2 - Paperback

Printed in the United States of America 1 2 0 9 1 9

♾This paper meets the requirements of ANSI/NISO Z39.48-1992 (Permanence of Paper)

Unless otherwise noted, all scripture is taken from the Holy Bible, King James Version (Public Domain).

For Mattie, the one that made me a mom and Bryan a dad. The one that has a quiet faith in God. The one that has sat on the sidelines of much of this journey cheering everyone on without any recognition. The one that is so special, it would take a whole other book to explain. You are precious! You are our favorite girl in the whole wide world, and we love you to the beach and back a billion times!

[1]Wherefore seeing we also are compassed about with so great a cloud of witnesses, let us lay aside every weight, and the sin which doth so easily beset us, and let us run with patience the race that is set before us, [2]Looking unto Jesus the author and finisher of our faith; who for the joy that was set before him endured the cross, despising the shame, and is set down at the right hand of the throne of God.

—Hebrews 12: 1–2

CONTENTS

PREFACE

And we know that all things work together for good to them that love God, to them who are the called according to his purpose.

—Romans 8:28

First of all, I can't take credit for anything good in this book. Yes, this has been my life for the last forty-something years, *but God* gave me a story to tell. So, all credit and glory should be given to God.

With that said, if my story doesn't make any sense or you hate it, well, that is on me. I'm not a writer, and I had no idea how to begin writing a book in the first place. *But God* has been crafting this master plan for so long. He has brought our family to the public eye in such outstanding ways in the last year. It is obvious that He is using us in a major spiritual way.

So much has happened in our lives that it was hard to decide which point of view to tell this story from. Such viewpoints could have been my family as a whole, including my husband, Bryan, my daughter, Mattie, my son, Max, and of course myself, Lori; or my husband and I only. Would the focus of the book be on my son's health concerns? I'm sure my daughter could tell a very different story in how this has impacted her. Then, what would I call the book? *The Race*? *The Journey*? Where does one even begin trying to explain how God has worked such a story plot that even the most creative screenwriter could create? All these things ran through my head as I sat in the hospital with my son after his brain-tumor diagnosis. God had given us a big story to tell, and I had so many questions.

I guess I should start by telling you that several months prior to my son's brain-tumor diagnosis, something told me I needed to write a book about how God had been working in my life. He had answered so many prayers for me that I, overwhelmed, felt like I should tell everyone how great He was. I told God, "If you want me to write a book, you are going to have to send me some major signs, because that is totally out of my comfort zone. I don't even like to read that much!"

Almost immediately, I was given a sign. One day as I sat in my car at the mall reading over my to-do list for the day, the thought that God had given me about writing a book came back into my mind. As I was explaining to Him in my head that I would need some major signs, I happened to look up from my phone and saw a sign! I had no idea I was sitting in front of the mall bookstore.

When God's signs come to me, I always know they are from Him; I can just feel it. This wave of overwhelming awe hits me like a strong wind coming out of nowhere on the beach. I just remember thinking God was still crazy to choose me to write a book, but agreed to be willing if He gave me more direction and more of a story to tell. Boy, did He ever.

A few months knocked along, and my son's brain-tumor journey began right after his preacher-calling journey (I will get to all that). It appeared to our family that God was *really* trying to get our attention, and that God had some kind of job for Max or us to do. Things just started falling into place, and our job was to just have faith, wait, and be obedient. Sound easy? Well, it actually kind of was! I hope that I can put it all into words that make sense.

It wasn't until my friend and hairdresser Erika and I were having a quick root-coloring session before my son and I set out on an eight-week journey for radiation treatments that I realized

God was seriously wanting me to write this book sooner than I thought. As usual, we were catching up on the most recent ways God had been showing up and showing out in my life. This seemed to be our topic for the last several sessions. So, as I was telling her the most recent "God moments," she (what I thought was jokingly at first) said, "You need to write a book about this journey God has your family on."

I laughed at her. She told me she wasn't joking. She told me so many people were waiting to see each day how God is using us for His glory. I told her it was funny that she said that, because our preacher, Jason, had delivered a message the day before (our only church service since being home from the hospital) about Hebrews 11 and 12. He specifically spoke to my little family when he read, actually turning and addressing us personally as he talked about this scripture:

> [1]*Wherefore seeing we also are compassed about with so great a cloud of witnesses, let us lay aside every weight, and the sin which doth so easily beset us, and let us run with patience the race that is set before us,* [2]*Looking unto Jesus the author and finisher of our faith; who for the joy that was set before him endured the cross, despising the shame, and is set down at the right hand of the throne of God.*
>
> —Hebrews 12: 1–2

He talked about our family and how people were watching how we handled ourselves in this "race" God had "set before us." He told us to "keep our faith," "be patient," "be joyful," and "be a light for others." Joy had been kind of a big thing to me since our church camp the summer right before we found the tumor. I will explain more about that later, but to be joyous while your son is sick and about to go through a difficult part of the journey is something you don't typically expect to be.

But God had led us to somehow find joy in this journey, or race. Our preacher went on to say that in order to finish a race, you have to be patient, pace yourself, and look to God. He talked about life and how it's not always easy. He used Jesus as an example. Jesus's life wasn't always easy, and he specifically discussed when Jesus died on the cross. He quoted John 3:16: "For God so loved the world, that he gave his only begotten Son, that whosoever believeth in him should not perish, but have everlasting life."

John 3:16 has been an important verse to us for some time now, not only as Christians, but due to the fact that the verse is where Max got his dirt-bike racing number from; he was #316. He came up with that all on his own a few years before he got sick, before he knew he had been called to preach, before he knew he had a tumor, and before our life went crazy.

So, when Jason went on to say that if God loved His only son so much and didn't help get him out of the situation he was in on the cross (when God obviously had the power to do that), and we are no better, I got chills. Just because God can make problems go away, it doesn't mean that He will do that when He needs to use us for something that is bigger than our current, sometimes painful situation. Before that day, I'd never thought about trials in that way. He made it so clear to me that I'm definitely in no way better than Jesus, and if Jesus had to die on the cross to be used by God for salvation for you and me, then my life being shaken up and changed around is actually something to be seen as a blessing, not a series of unfortunate events. Wow. That was pretty deep!

The best part about the whole message, though, was when he said he had had it on his heart for weeks, and God had kept telling him to wait before he preached on it. God wouldn't allow him to use that message until we were there to hear it. Due to the tumor and all that was going on, we hadn't been to church in a few weeks. God had sent that message just for us, my family. Wow. That's pretty overwhelming, isn't it? It is to me.

I'd heard messages before that I felt were directed toward me, but never had I had a preacher speak specifically to me in a time in my life where my faith was being tested so severely. It came at just the right time, and I'm so thankful to Jason for being so obedient. A message given to the wrong crowd can fall on deaf ears, but my ears were definitely perked up that Sunday. I was suddenly focused even more on this journey in which we were entered.

Erika and I continued talking about all the ways God had used my son and our family to show how great and powerful He is. She again told me that I needed to write a book, and she even offered to help me. I laughed. She didn't; she was serious. I told her there was no way I could even begin to explain in words all the great plot twists and details of this journey we are on. She said it's more like a race. "You should call it 'The Race,'" she told me.

That thought stopped me in my tracks, because so much of my life has revolved around some type of racing or competition. I dated a racecar driver; I played sports up until my kids were born; my brother raced cars for fun briefly; my husband raced dirt bikes; my mom was a half-marathon fanatic; and my son raced dirt bikes.

But once again, I blew her off. However, I did think to myself, *I do feel like this would make a great book, if someone could tell the story better than me. God, if you want me to actually write a book, you will have to have someone blatantly tell me to do it. It needs to be so obvious that it is from YOU. Otherwise, I'm not doing it.*

As I left the salon to get in my car, Erika poked her head out the door and said very sternly, as if it wasn't even coming from her, "Write the book! Call it 'The Race.' You need to share your story!" Well, that was just another moment when God made it clear to me what I probably needed to do. Still, though, I didn't feel qualified or worthy to write this story. I still wasn't sure if it was something I could even do. I thought, *God, you are losing it!* I think I even said that out loud as I put my car in reverse.

Later that night, my husband, son, and I were hanging out, talking. We were talking about how God had been in this journey from the beginning, and how much better Max was feeling. We talked about how amazing his recovery was (again, I will explain more later), and how many people had prayed and seen prayers answered (yep, more information later). I told them that Erika had told me I should write a book. My husband, the most unlikely person to want our life story available for the public, tells me, "You know, we can joke about that, but it is definitely something to think about. We and Max definitely have a story to tell."

I thought to myself, *God, you have done it. You have found the right person to encourage me.* You see, such a statement felt unlikely for Bryan, because ever since social media became such a prominent part of our culture, he has adamantly said, nearly on a daily basis, "Don't put me on the 'interweb.' I mean it!" So, for him to seriously say that we should write a book telling people how God has worked in our lives blew me away. And he was serious!

So, I suppose God really, *really* wants this book to be written. I'm going to attempt to tell this story about this "race" He has entered us in, but you need to know that I do not feel capable, qualified, or worthy. I love the saying "God doesn't call the qualified; he qualifies the called." Here goes . . .

CHAPTER ONE

THE START

That if thou shalt confess with thy mouth the Lord Jesus, and shalt believe in thine heart that God hath raised him from the dead, thou shalt be saved.

—Romans 10:9

The start—that is the beginning of anything. In racing, specifically the off-road dirt-bike racing which my son takes part in, there is always a lot of work put in that leads up to the start of the race. That is probably the most important part of racing: getting everything ready. So, the "work" that leads up to the part of this book you are probably most interested in is just as important. Our start was where God was getting us ready for this big race in our life. So, I need to include some history before we jump right into the actual "tumor race" itself.

I guess it all started when I was born. Just kidding; I'm not going to go that far back, but I do need to give my background, including my testimony.

I grew up in a very small town in North Georgia called Dawsonville. It's grown a lot since I was younger. Back then, everyone knew everyone. There were very few restaurants, and we had to drive forever to get to a mall. We had—and still have—quite a few churches in our county. Only in the last ten years have our stores been allowed sell alcohol on Sundays. When I was growing up, everyone helped everyone, and that is still true today. It is just a great place to have grown up and to continue raising my family as I have gotten older.

My mom and dad are awesome parents. They both served different purposes in my life. Daddy was the one who drove hours to work each day to provide the things we needed, and he was the one that we liked to take shopping, because he let us get whatever we wanted. He also provided a great ear when we had problems, but most of all, he kept the humor in our lives. To know him is to love him and laugh with him.

My mom was the one that kept our schedule going, and three kids aren't easy to coordinate. We all played various sports and were all involved in a lot of things. She worked, too, so she had to coordinate rides for us to all of our events. She also made sure we had the things we needed. Maybe not all that we wanted, but she definitely worked overtime on the part of getting us what we needed.

One of the things she thought we needed was God. She was right. She dragged us to church even when we didn't want to go. I didn't like her much on those mornings, but I went anyway. I'm so glad she made us go, because that is how I came to know God.

She arranged for us to attend things at church while she was working. One of those was the Vacation Bible School (VBS) at Concord Baptist Church in Silver City, Georgia. Since both Mama and Daddy were working, we rode a school bus the church sent to pick up kids. So it was, as an eight-year-old girl at VBS, my life changed.

I don't remember too much about the week, but I do recall it was during the day in the summer. My older cousin, Andi, had gotten saved recently. She was trying to tell me about it one night at my Granny and Papa's house. At that time, I didn't really know what being saved meant; I just knew that she said I had to be saved to get to Heaven. I knew enough about Hell to know that I didn't want to go there, so on the last day of our VBS when they gave the altar call, something different was going on in my heart that I couldn't explain and didn't really understand. It wasn't until one of the ladies of the church came to me and asked if I was lost that I realized I *was* lost and needed to be saved. I took one step with her out of the pew, knowing in my heart that I was lost and wanted God to save me, and instantly felt better. I really didn't know what to pray when we got to the altar, because I already felt saved by the time I walked down there. Years later, I realized it was because I *was* saved when I took that first step. That first step toward the altar acknowledged that I believed Jesus had died on the cross for me, and I needed him to guide the rest of my life. God knew my heart.

However, about eight years later as a sixteen-year-old girl helping with a class in VBS, I began to doubt my salvation. I asked myself, *Could it really have been that easy? Could God save me when I just learned that I was lost?* I had to go to the altar to find out. As soon as I took that step out toward the altar, God told me I was, in fact, saved as an eight-year-old girl. I was super shy, so instead of turning back around and going back to my seat, I continued to the altar and pretended to pray. I was so embarrassed to tell people that I was already saved that I went through with getting rebaptized! I would rather be baptized again than have to talk to people and explain what was really going on. So, I got baptized again. Double-dipped is better than never-dipped, I guess.

From that point on, God was always an important part of my life. He always guided me, even if I didn't always listen. The greatest part was when I didn't listen and took matters into my own hands, He was always there welcoming me back in to do things His way. Always forgiving.

Chapter Two

The Rose

But they that wait upon the Lord shall renew their strength; they shall mount up with wings as eagles; they shall run, and not be weary; and they shall walk, and not faint.

—Isaiah 40:31

Now, let's flash forward a few years and get to the part where I met my future husband, favorite boyfriend, and best friend. From the time Bryan and I found each other, God had big plans for us, and I knew that. It was something that I felt, but couldn't explain. I had known who Bryan was for a long time. He also grew up in Dawsonville, Georgia, but we lived on complete opposite ends of the county. Our paths didn't cross very often. I was into sports; he was into dirt-bike racing and working.

I do remember seeing him one time when my parents were building our house. He had come to deliver lumber or materials. His family owned—and actually still owns—a building-supply company that furnishes materials for custom homes. He was standing in our new house looking out the door toward our doublewide trailer that we lived in at the time. It was in the front yard of the new house. I remember thinking he was really cute, but that's about as far as my thoughts went on Bryan Grant at twelve or thirteen years old.

Our paths never really crossed socially until my senior year in high school. I started dating his best friend, Casey. I didn't date Casey very long, but long enough to figure out what type of guy I wanted long term. Casey was a great guy: funny, always smiling, always positive, always fun, always kind, always made you feel special. I would soon learn that Bryan was just like him, but even more perfect for me.

Casey was diagnosed with cancer right after we started dating. He and I dated most of my senior year, but Casey decided that dating wasn't what was best for us while he was dealing with his cancer battle. It broke my heart, but I could see in his eyes that it was breaking his to let me go, too. He was very wise, and looking back on it now, I know he was following what God was telling him to do. He told me once that his mom would read Isaiah 40:31 to him at night and that was what kept him going. It's funny how that verse would later resurface to be so important in my life.

A couple of years passed. I dated people, and so did Bryan. We had some of the same friends, and our paths crossed occasionally. We even hung out in the same friend group occasionally. Casey battled cancer for about two of those years, and eventually it took his life. It wasn't until then that I was able to see Bryan in a different light. He loved Casey so much, and so did I. Everyone that knew him loved him. Casey's death devastated us all, including the professional car-racing circuit. He was Bill Elliott's nephew, and had been one of the up-and-coming young racers to watch. Besides Casey's family, Bryan was the one most affected. He lost his very best friend in the world. The day of Casey's funeral, Bryan spoke about what a great person his friend had been. I can't remember exactly what he said, but I will never forget thinking what strength it took for Bryan to get up there in front of hundreds of people and speak about someone he loved so much. I admired him for that speech.

After the funeral, some of us friends met back up at the funeral home, where we had left our cars so we could ride together to the cemetery. As I was going to mine, Bryan pulled up beside me and let me choose from two flowers he had gotten off the arrangements from Casey's grave. I chose the rose. Bryan getting that flower from the grave showed me how thoughtful he was. I would never have thought of taking a flower, and definitely wouldn't have thought to give it to someone else. It's weird how you can see goodness in tragedy, good in sad times; how the worst day can end up being one of your best. You'll see that later on, God will bring Bryan and I together again for another day kind of like that. Through our sadness, somehow we became best friends.

Not long after Casey passed away, Bryan and I decided to start dating. It's funny how God works. I had never even really thought of Bryan Grant as someone I would ever date, yet something drew us together like two magnets. Thankfully, like always, God knew what He was doing! He was that magnetic force I felt!

A rose was kind of our "thing" for many years. He would get me roses for Valentine's Day, including a ceramic rose one year. The cards we gave each other always had a rose or a bunch of roses. That's how it was . . . until the kids came along. Then, everything changed!

Chapter Three

The Kids

For this child I prayed; and the Lord hath given me my petition which I asked of him.

—1 Samuel 1:27

Bryan and I dated for five years. I knew I wanted to marry him around year one. From the beginning, his family took me in like their very own child. They loved me like my own parents did. That made it even easier for me to see a bright future with Bryan.

He is a cautious thinker and never rushes into big decisions. So, to say that he took his time to ask me to marry him is an understatement. But, it was totally worth the wait!

We got married in 2001 in Jamaica, and it was the best decision for our personalities and relationship. My only regret is not planning to wed in Jamaica in time to have our families with us. We had a big party when we got back home, but I will always wish our parents, siblings, and best friends could've experienced our wedding with us instead of watching a video of it when we got back home. With that said, our day was *ours,* and it was perfect for us.

We had our first baby, Mattie, a little over a year after we got married. I prayed that God would help us guide our kids and be good parents. I prayed that our kids would be wise and cautious, and love Jesus like Bryan and I do. Well, they are and they do.

My pregnancy with Mattie Elizabeth Grant was effortless. I wasn't sick and didn't have any craziness during her pregnancy. I loved being pregnant! I loved her from the first little flutter I felt when she started moving. She loved church even from the womb, doing flips the whole time the choir sang. Her delivery was smooth. In fact, everything about her is smooth and gentle (for the most part!).

Mattie is such a spitting image of me. She looks like me, acts like me, thinks like me. We have the same sense of humor. She's like her daddy in lots of ways, too. She's tidy and organized like him (you should see my closet). She is a good blend of the two of us, I think. She's been such a great big sister to Max—a way better big sister than I ever was. She had her sixteenth birthday in the hospital, because it was three days after Max's brain surgery. That was a choice she made. Bless her heart. Every year we plan something for her birthday, there's something that causes us to have to change her party. She is a class act, though, and just goes with the flow. She's just an amazing daughter, sister, and friend. She's kind to all and never has a bad thing to say about anyone. These verses remind me of her so much:

> *Strength and honour are her clothing; and she shall rejoice in time to come.*
> [26]*She openeth her mouth with wisdom; and in her tongue is the law of kindness.*
>
> —Proverbs 31:25

She loves God and going to church. She may be too shy to show it often, but she loves people and being kind. She's my little best-friend gift from God. The day she was born is one I will never forget. As I held her for the first time and Bryan looked into her eyes, she blinked so slowly, as if to say, "I can't believe you are my mom and dad." That's how we felt, too: instantly in love. A love that is indescribable to those who have never experienced having a child. I had always heard that I would love her like no love I'd ever felt. I remember thinking to myself, *How can you possibly love someone any differently than the people you already love so much in your life?* Well, you can. I did. We did, and still do.

We loved Mattie so much that we wanted to be sure she had a sibling, a best friend for life, a brother or sister. My sister was three years younger than me, and my brother was eight years younger. We were close as siblings, but not so close that we had the same friend groups. My brother's friend group was way younger than me, and my sister's just young enough to not really have anything in common until high school, really. I wanted my kids to be even closer. So, when Mattie was almost one year old, we decided to give her a sibling.

From early on in the pregnancy with Max, strange things started happening. One thing after another landed us in the hospital late at night from some random, weird, but not serious thing. Around twenty-eight weeks, one of those things was the reason we found out I was having contractions. I didn't feel them, so I had no idea. They put me on medication to stop them, but by thirty-seven weeks, I had been on bedrest for two weeks and was miserable. I was hurting, uncomfortable, and still having contractions. So, after an amniocentesis to see if Max's lungs were developed, I went into full-blown labor. Luckily, his little lungs were developed enough that we had ourselves a bouncing baby boy we were able to take home after the normal two-day hospital stay. We had a son we named Max Lee Grant. Mattie had a baby brother. Life was good.

Around three weeks into Max's life, he started projectile

vomiting. If you've ever seen the movie *The Exorcist*, then you can imagine what I'm talking about. It was bad . . . so bad. Like, change-clothes-three-times-before-you-even-get-in-the-car-to-go-somewhere kind of bad. Like, don't-burp-him-over-your-shoulder-in-church-because-he's-going-to-get-the-people-behind-you bad. We tried lots of medicines, chiropractors, food changes. Nothing seemed to help. He cried day and night. There was no position or amount of love that could keep him from throwing up and crying.

After about three months, the crying suddenly stopped. It was the first day he stayed with Mrs. Dena, the babysitter, and the first day I went back to work after he was born. *Maybe I caused his reflux somehow? Maybe the tumor was forming then?* Only God knows the answer to those questions. What I do know is that I am so glad he stopped crying, because we *loved* Mrs. Dena, and I was so afraid she would kick him out because he cried so much. After about six months, the vomiting stopped. It was really weird. We will never know if that had anything to do with the tumor or not.

Max has always been such a loving child. He takes that after his daddy. He looks just like his daddy, too. In so many ways he is like my brother, Ethan, though. He is mischievous and likes to play jokes. From early on, we could see he had an old soul. Everyone who knows him says that about him. He liked to cuddle, snuggle, and give kisses from the start. He was the one who would run in from playing outside just so he could hug me. When he was in the fifth grade, he still held my hand when we walked together. I asked him if he would please always let me hold his hand, even when he got older (like when he became a teenager). He said he would, and he still does. He also still likes to curl up with us on the couch sometimes. He still likes to give hugs. He will even hug me at school! He has always marched to the beat of his own drum and doesn't really care so much about what others think. Everyone who knows him loves that about him.

Max was also the one that had all the ear infections, broken arms, heart condition, and asthma. Bless his heart. He asks me all the time why he's the one with all the issues. I just tell him he's special. Later in this book, you'll get to hear his take on just how special he really is. God told me a long time ago that Max was going to be used in a special way. I had no idea just how special until recently.

CHAPTER FOUR

THE RACING

But none of these things move me, neither count I my life dear unto myself, so that I might finish my course with joy, and the ministry, which I have received of the Lord Jesus, to testify the gospel of the grace of God.

—Acts 20:24

It seems racing has been a major part of mine and Bryan's life since even before we met. Bryan had been part of Casey's pit crew before he passed away. Had he not gotten cancer, he probably would've made it all the way to NASCAR, just like his Uncle Bill. His cousin, Chase, Bill's son born right before Casey passed away, races NASCAR now. Casey would've been so proud. Bryan cheers Chase on just like I think Casey would've. It is a little piece of Casey that Bryan can hang onto.

When we first started dating, Bryan raced dirt bikes, and we traveled all over going to races. I even went to a twenty-four-hour race in Alabama when I was about six months pregnant with Mattie. It was miserably hot. We slept in a racing trailer on cots, and we had no bathroom. Y'all, that's love. I must really love this guy!

From an early age, we wanted our kids to be involved in sports or some kind of activity to get them to be social. For Mattie, it started out with clogging and soccer. I even helped coach soccer for two years. One year, I helped with Mattie's team, and one year I helped Mattie's *and* Max's teams. I had only played basketball and softball growing up. Needless to say, I was not the best soccer coach. At the ages of four and six, you really don't need to know a whole lot except "kick it" and "run." We learned the rest along the way from other coaches. We really didn't care if the kids did well, as long as they improved and had fun.

Then, Mattie moved on to basketball. It seemed like that was going to be her thing. She enjoyed it, and with some lessons became way more confident and had a beautiful shot! One coach called her "Auto-Mattie," because she had this one sweet spot on the wing that was her best shot that almost never missed. She usually missed the first two, but then got the shot dialed in for the rest of the game. We loved watching her play.

In tenth grade, she decided she was done with basketball and was going to try cross country. We laughed, because her least favorite part of basketball was the end of practice when the team had to run. But, cross country seemed to be something that made her happy. It was drama-free, and she was really only competing against herself for a better time. She liked it, so we liked it.

The summer that Max told his preacher calling, and also the "tumor summer," she asked if she could quit cross country. Typically, I would have encouraged her to stick it out, but this year something was different. I just didn't feel compelled to make her keep running if she didn't want to do it. It was not my normal response, *but God* must've been in charge of that one. He knew that our life was about to change drastically, and didn't allow her quitting to affect me like it normally would've. I was fine with it. It seemed like the right thing to do. So strange, but it did.

It ended up that I wouldn't have been able to go to any of her meets had she stuck with it, anyway. That would've devastated both of us. I didn't miss anything my kids were doing—ever. Since I was a teacher, it was pretty easy for me to attend all of their ball games and events.

Max played soccer, baseball, and basketball for several years. He played football for two years, but it wasn't his favorite. Around the age of nine or ten, he decided that racing was his favorite. He had been riding around the house since he was about four, and had been in a few races along the way. Once he fell in love with racing, all other sports went out the window.

Bryan and I tried to get him to play at least one team sport each year, so during his seventh grade year he decided he would try cross country. It was really hard for him. He has asthma and a heart condition that causes his heart to get out of rhythm. Then, there was all the throwing up that had started, but he tried his best, anyway. We were proud of him for his perseverance. He ran again in eighth grade. During that year, if he wasn't throwing up before the race, his heart or asthma were acting up. That became what just a normal day looked like for him at that point.

He really shined in the dirt-bike racing. He worked so hard riding with his older racing buddies, trying to get faster. Bryan was the pit crew and mechanic who made the bike the best it could be, and he made sure Max always had a good bike to ride. He taught Max everything he knew about racing. Bryan is a great teacher, and Max soaked it all in. Eventually, he was one of the kids you wanted to watch at the races, especially in the last few years. He had gotten so much faster!

Our life revolved around racing for the 2017 race season, Max's eighth-grade year. Bryan and Max went to every race they could find. Mattie and I would go to most of them, but sometimes we stayed home to go to church. We always felt so bad missing church. That year, I gave up my Sunday school class to focus on watching Max race. That was out of the ordinary for me, but something inside me told me that I needed to do that. I loved my Sunday school class, but the church had made some changes in how the classes were set up, so it just seemed like a good time to let it go. I was able to do so without feeling like I had disappointed God, too. That was the strangest part.

Now, I know that God had his hand in that, also. He knew that my life was about to change drastically, and I had to be separated from that duty to fulfill another. He also knew that I wouldn't be able to live with myself if I hadn't been there for Max as much as possible that last year of racing before we found the tumor.

So, basically, our life went from racing when we had time to completely revolving around a racing schedule for over a year in 2017 and 2018. So much so, we were at a race when the first sign of the tumor appeared. Being at that race instead of church would later be something that I went from regretting to being thankful for.

Chapter Five

The Church

For where two or three are gathered together in my name, there am I in the midst of them.

—Matthew 18:20

First of all, I need to tell you that our county has several sweet little churches. Many of them took us in as their church family during our journey. They prayed for us like we were their very own. I will forever be grateful to them.

We attend the best little church on the side of the road: Bethel Baptist Church of Dawsonville, Georgia. It is small, but we do great things. Most of our members are related to someone in the church somehow and live within a ten-mile radius of our church. We've gained several new members over the last few years—so many new members, in fact, that they added onto the church while we were on this tumor journey. It was as though as God healed Max, he was creating more room for people to be a part of our church.

About ten years ago, I felt like God was calling me to work for him. I had no idea what that would entail, but I can remember the night I prayed on my living-room floor to get direction from God. I waited until the kids went to bed and I was alone. I prayed that God would guide me in whatever it was he wanted me to do.

In God's fashion, I had to wait several months to find out what it was He wanted me to do. But, when the Sunday school superintendent called and asked me to teach Sunday school, I knew I couldn't say no. I was terrified, because I didn't know the Bible like I felt like I should, but I said yes anyway. Through that assignment, I've learned the Bible much better than what I used to know. I still have so much to learn, but teaching Sunday school was such a blessing to me. I have had various opportunities to serve God through our church, and am so thankful for each and every one. I got a blessing and grew so much as a Christian from each assignment.

Our biggest outreach each year is in December. We perform a live nativity scene outside around the back of our church. People come from all over to see it. Even when it is thirty degrees outside, we run tractor hayrides from 6:00 p.m. until 10:00–11:00 p.m. for two nights in December. It is such a blessing to be a part of this program each year, freezing temperatures, rain, snow, and all. You get on a hayride and bundle up for an hour to hear the story of Jesus from the beginning, when the angel comes to Mary in a dream, to the end, when Jesus rises from the tomb.

Our assignments for the last few years have been as follows: Mattie sings in the manger scene, I am a disciple (with a beard) in the Last Supper scene, Max is a soldier in the crucifixion scene, and Bryan is a shuttle driver in the parking lot. We all love to participate in this each year. Max's scene is fairly new, and Tracey Phillips, our nativity director, is to be credited for that idea. I can't begin to explain the feeling you get when you see the soldiers placing Jesus on the cross and piercing his side. When Mary, his mother, starts crying at the sight of her son on the cross, I cry every time. It is such a moving scene. I can't imagine having to watch your child be crucified and tortured in such a hateful manner.

I thought of Mary often as we entered the hospital. Seeing Max in that hospital bed post-surgery almost broke me, and we had the best-case scenario. (I promise I will get to that eventually.) Sometimes, the only thing that got me through the day was thinking, *It could be so much worse. I could be watching him be crucified on a cross and not be able to hold him in my arms, or hug him, or talk to him.*

Our VBS is the third week in June and always has a great turnout. For the last several years, Bryan and I have helped with the teen class at VBS. It has been such a blessing to get to see our own kids, their friends, and kids their age speak out about God and what He has done for them. We usually have a speaker come for at least one lesson so the kids don't get tired of hearing us. Each year we get such a blessing.

For the last three years, we have helped Andy Wallace with the teens. He has been a longtime friend to both of us. Andy rents an outdoor event tent for our class, because there are so many teens. More than forty teens in one of our small Sunday school rooms just doesn't work that well, and in years past, they needed the big room for another class. The teens are the easiest group to manage outside, so to the tent we went. It was cool, though. They liked it. So, having a preacher coming to speak to a tent class seemed almost like a tent revival, especially since we were on the side of the road!

Our church is always doing things like that to try to get the youth excited about something. We don't have fancy coffee, fancy sound equipment, or a band, but we do get a tent once a year. That is why I love our church so much: we don't need fancy, just God's spirit and loving people to put it all together.

A few years ago, we started going to church camp. I have been so blessed to be a part of the church camp committee since it was started. It is amazing to me how God works. Each year, the theme has been sent to the committee from God, and each year, it couldn't be more perfect. One year it was about being like a pineapple: standing tall, wearing a crown, and being sweet on the inside. The summer before that theme, every store I went into had pineapples on everything—shirts, paper plates, tote bags, everything. God always sends signs to us that we are on the right track!

At our 2018 church camp, the theme was watermelons and planting seeds. Of course, as expected, God sent us watermelons everywhere we turned when we went shopping. Even the outlet mall in our county had watermelons on the advertisements. We found so many watermelon items in each store. The crazy thing is, when God sends us the themes, they are always in the fall—almost a year before our church camp. So, we weren't getting inspirations from what we were seeing out during that time, but instead we were getting signs a year later that we were on the right track.

One of the services in 2018 was led by a young preacher named Sam Castleberry, a twenty-year-old who had helped our preacher in a revival earlier that summer. He had told his preacher calling in June, just like Max. It was August now. He had been preaching for roughly two months, and he did such a great job. Our speakers and preachers always do great jobs, but his message carried so much weight with me. It was about joy. He talked about when you have God in your life, and with Jesus as your personal savior, you can experience such great joy—more joy than anything else in this world can give you. He talked about the difference between joy and happiness. He said happiness is temporary. Lots of things can give you temporary happiness, but God gives you joy that can be there even when you are going through something difficult. If you are saved and have a relationship with God, no matter what trials you are going through, you can find joy.

Wow. I had no idea how much his message would help me in my future walk.

When we left that service, I ran across a rock garden at the facility we use for our church camp. I had never noticed it before. Several rocks were painted with inspirational sayings. The biggest rock caught my eye, not because it was the biggest, but because it had a single word covering the entire rock painted on it that stopped me in my tracks: Joy.

God had gone and wowed me again!

I wouldn't understand just how much that message would be needed in my life until a week or so later, but I knew it was stuck in my mind for a reason.

Chapter Six

The Storm Delay

[3]And not only so, but we glory in tribulations also: knowing that tribulation worketh patience; [4]And patience, experience; and experience, hope.

—Romans 5:3–4

It's rare, but sometimes there would be a storm delay or even a cancellation in Max's racing world. Although we had no idea we had entered into a spiritual race of our own at the time, the onset of tumor symptoms would be our storm delay.

Max wrote an essay for his online school (post–tumor removal) that was spot-on for our journey. In it, he talked about the very first time we saw symptoms of a tumor: May 21, 2017. We had no idea they were tumor symptoms at the time.

As I mentioned before, he had been racing dirt bikes for some time. For his races, we camp on Saturday in a big pasture or field where the races are held, and he races on Sunday. Everyone camps. There are at least one hundred campers in the fields. I bet locals wonder what is going on when they drive by the races. It really is a sight to see!

Sometime after midnight on that May Sunday morning, there was a huge thunderstorm. The thunder was so loud that it woke everyone in the area up. We all jumped up to check outside, because we just knew it had hit someone's camper near us. We looked out to make sure our friends in the camper beside us were not going up in flames. The booming of the thunder and the striking of the lightning were the loudest and closest I have ever heard in my life. I've always heard that thunder was a rumbling from God in Heaven. I guess we could've taken that as our first sign that God was up to something in our lives.

It really was that loud and memorable. I can still hear the *BOOM!* in my head.

We finally went back to sleep with the storm still going, but settling a little. Max woke up to get ready to race around 7:00 a.m. and started throwing up. He was so sick. We thought it was something he had eaten or a stomach bug, but like in show business, the show must go on. He decided to race anyway.

He won the race, so that should show you how much determination and dedication he had in his racing career. He wanted to go pro. That's all he had talked about for several years. I think God's thunder was the beginning of a life-altering path for Max.

He continued throwing up every morning for about two weeks. He felt pretty lousy throughout the day, but still went to school to finish the year. We thought it was a food allergy or something at first. When we noticed it was only occurring in the morning, Max really thought it was something he was eating. Yet, when we changed his diet and it didn't change the vomiting, we knew something was wrong.

I took him to the doctor in early June 2017. He was diagnosed with reflux and put on an over-the-counter medication. We were also asked to keep a food journal and change his diet for a month. Max ate a pretty bland diet already, so we pretty much just had to eliminate dairy and fried foods. We kept the journal like they had asked.

Although he felt awful, Max started cross country that summer and would throw up almost every day before he ran. He continued cross country and racing dirt bikes the rest of that summer and fall, all while still throwing up. At this point, we had contacted the doctor a few times, and she had changed his reflux medication brand and time of day a few times.

Although he had some good days, there were lots of bad. In September 2017, he got the "stomach bug" twice: once when we took a trip to Ohio to go to the Cedar Point roller coasters, and again when Hurricane Irma devastated our state. On the day that Irma rolled through our county, Max was vomiting hourly. It was pitiful. We had a house full of kids who had gotten "Irmacaned" in and couldn't go home, so I had to quarantine him, thinking he had a stomach bug again. We just thought his immune system was low or he was just unlucky. It always passed after twelve to twenty-four hours. The only time it went on longer was the original instance in May when we were thinking it was a food allergy.

By December 2017, he was still throwing up. Not every day, but enough to make him feel pretty lousy almost all the time. He was still trying to do all the things he loved. We were still trying different combinations of his over-the-counter reflux medications. But, by the end of December 2017 and beginning of January 2018, when Christmas break was coming to an end, he started to feel really bad. Up until this point, he had not let the vomiting slow him down at all. But, this was different. I noticed he started napping a lot, not eating much at all, losing weight, and getting very pale. Something just wasn't right. He hadn't taken a nap since he was three years old.

We went to Wyoming to visit Bryan's cousin and his family. They took us skiing. It was New Year's, so we were trying to do fun things, but Max was just not himself. He was really quiet, too. I could tell he was worried.

When we got home, I called the doctor and asked that we be sent to a specialist. I felt like seven months of nothing working was plenty enough to show we had done our part at home. They sent us to a gastroenterologist in Atlanta. After a visit where we mostly talked about the frequency and consistency of Max's poop and food changes, the doctor decided an endoscopy was in order. Well, this led to a discussion about Max's heart condition. Apparently, you have to be careful when using anesthesia if you have a heart condition. So, we had to see the cardiologist before we could work on his stomach issues any further.

Thankfully, I was able to get Max in with the cardiologist the next day. He put Max on a heart monitor in order to track his arrhythmias, but cleared him for the endoscopy. Finally, we were on our way to an answer.

The endoscopy went well and nothing looked suspicious. The gastroenterologist put Max on a medication to help his stomach empty out food in case that wasn't happening, which could've been causing the reflux. At first, we thought the medication was the answer to our prayers. We had been dealing with this vomiting situation for almost a year at that point. The new medication seemed to help . . . for about a month.

Suddenly, the vomiting started again, and we had a new symptom: dizziness. Just great. Bless his heart. He felt so bad, and he tried to continue with all the things he'd previously loved, but it's hard to get up, throw up, and race with very little energy. Also by this point, he had thrown up all of his favorite foods, so he pretty much hated all foods. That became another bump in the road.

At this time, the dizziness wasn't happening all the time. He usually only mentioned it after riding his dirt bike and jumping jumps. The vomiting was the major issue. It would stop for a few days, then come back full force. Just when we thought we had figured out which food or eating pattern was causing it, he would throw up and blow that philosophy. We thought the new nausea medication was causing the dizziness, as it was a possible side effect. We honestly paid the dizziness little attention until the summer.

By June 2018, we were a full year into this "treatment plan." Max was frustrated. I was frustrated. He was wanting to go on a trip with the teen boys at our church to one of our member's homes in Colorado out in the middle of nowhere. I was so nervous about Max's vomiting, but he insisted on going. So, we planned on letting him go . . . on a trip . . . without us . . . to the middle of nowhere . . . throwing up . . . and barely eating.

That sounds like a great plan, doesn't it?

Chapter Seven

The Green Flag

Study to shew thyself approved unto God, a workman that needeth not to be ashamed, rightly dividing the word of truth.

—2 Timothy 2

At Max's races, everyone waited for that first green flag. It immediately followed the prayer, the singing of the national anthem, and a unanimous engine-starting of the entire field of dirt bikes. That is probably my favorite part of the race, when all the racers seem to acknowledge their support of their country. The waving of the green flag is the beginning. It's when the race actually starts. I guess we had no idea ours had started until we were well into the race. *But God* did.

I called the group going to Colorado the Bethel Boys, since it was the teen boys and a few men from our church. Tracey, the nativity-scene coordinator, organized this trip, and it was his home in Colorado.

We got all the Bethel Boys prepped for the vomiting they were going to encounter on their trip. I told Tracey to just ignore Max and let him do his thing when he threw up; he'd be fine. He just needed to get it all out each morning and then he'd be good to go. Lanier, Bryan's cousin Amy's husband, a deacon of the church, and an EMT, was going on the trip, too. That made me feel much better. Both of his boys, Brendan and Bailey, were going. Brendan is not only Max's cousin, but also his best friend. I also prepped Lanier and Tracey on Max's diet, or lack thereof. He was down to eating almost nothing at this point. Tracey looked at me like, *What have I gotten myself into?* I assured him that Max would be fine, and the less attention drawn to him, the better.

I packed him a separate bag full of the snacks he was still able to eat. For a full year, we had worked our lives around Max's vomiting and lack of appetite so much that it was totally normal for me to get him a bag of food ready for this trip. I guess we really had been getting skilled in this area his whole life, though. Max is like his mama in the eating department: We like what we like and refuse to try what we think we won't like. But, this planning on vomiting and trying to find food he could still eat was getting very difficult. Packing a bag for Colorado was more difficult than an overnight bag for a friend's house. There was only room for a few of the foods that he likes to fit into a backpack, so I stocked up on those. I had to make sure he had enough for eight days. I filled his backpack full! It only had snacks in it, nothing else. I wasn't sure what they were planning to eat out in Colorado, but we were sure Max could survive on his snacks if he had to. I just prayed he didn't throw up so much he didn't want to eat at all. So, we were prepared for the worst, but we were letting him go anyway.

The trip was planned for the end of our 2018 VBS. Our VBS is Monday through Friday, starting the Monday after Father's Day each year. Bryan and I were helping with the teen class for VBS, and I was in charge of the message that Monday night. God had sent me a great message about a fishing pole. Here's what I typed up to share with the kids:

Analogy:

Fish - People you come in contact with daily and could bring to church
Bait - Your walk with God; what your friends see
Hook - J for Jesus; He's gotta be in it or it just won't work
Fishing line - Your prayers and talks with God; what your friends probably don't see
Fishing pole - Your testimony and faith; holds you up

The lesson was Luke 5:1–11, about how Peter had not wanted to go with Jesus and be a disciple at first. Peter continued his fishing. One day, Jesus saw Peter and his men fishing, and they weren't catching anything. Jesus told Peter to cast his net and a "great multitude of fishes" were in their net. Jesus knew that once Peter saw what great works He could do, Peter would then follow Him. That was our lesson: following Jesus's calling even when it is not necessarily what you thought your life would be like. It wasn't until just now, writing this book, that I realized how much weight that one lesson would have on my life.

The night I taught was the night Max told me some big news. The lesson was over. Since the VBS theme was "Moose on the Loose," the setting was a campsite. We don't even have moose in Georgia. The moose really isn't in the Bible or in the lessons. I didn't understand what a moose had to do with anything honestly, but we went with it. So, Andy (the same Andy who would later tell his own preacher calling), our fearless class leader who Bryan and I were assisting, had the idea for the kids to decorate their own camping chair. He found some that had sort of a plastic backing on the part you lean back on. A few dozen markers and forty-plus camp chairs later, we had ourselves a craft for the teens that they might actually use one day.

In order to decorate your chair, you had to have a partner to sit in the chair so you could bear down with your marker to decorate it. I partnered with Marley, our preacher's daughter. As she decorated her chair, I saw that Max had sent me a text. He was literally twelve feet away from me, so I wasn't sure why we was texting me.

Mama. Then another text came from him: *Mama, guess what.*

Well, by these two texts, I just thought he was being goofy because he didn't have to do a chair. We had made some examples over the weekend. Max had my artsy sister draw bigfoot on his. That goes with the VBS theme as much as a moose did, so I let him.

My phone was several feet away from me and I was trapped in the chair, so I didn't think much else of it and didn't respond. Shortly after that, the teens finished, we prayed, and we sent them to snacks.

Afterward, Bryan, Andy, and I cleaned up and stacked up the mound of chairs. I found my phone and looked to see what texts I had missed. I almost didn't look at the ones Max sent me since I thought he was being goofy. The only reason I checked them then was because I can't stand that red notification circle on my phone! I was clicking on all the texts I had received to make that red dot go away when I saw that Max had sent me one more after those first two: *I'm gonna be a preacher.*

Not many times in my life has something stopped me in my tracks. This text did, and it wasn't because I was surprised that Max was called to preach. I had felt like his life was headed in that direction for at least a year. He had asked some questions during our July 2017 revival that made it very clear to me that God was using him for something big. I had also noticed he had been separating himself from his friend group for the last couple of years, also. I guess it started sometime in sixth grade, and now going into ninth grade, I understood what exactly was going on. God had ahold of him. God had big plans for him. God had been working on this since Bryan and I met.

Wow! I had known those words would be coming at some point in Max's life. God had in His own way prepared me for that, but he had not prepared me for it happening when Max was fourteen. I know it is not something totally unheard of, but it is very rare that a fourteen-year-old tells his preacher calling.

If you are not a Baptist from the South, you may not understand what I mean when I say "preacher calling." I didn't realize that wasn't a common term until my son was called to preach. Baptists believe that God calls preachers in the sense that He gives you a purpose. You may be called to be a Sunday school teacher, or a deacon, piano player, singer, VBS director, etc. We don't really call those positions "called," but in order to explain it, I've had to rethink how I word it. I want to make it clear that it was not something Max chose for his job for God. Other types of churches may have people who choose to spread God's word on their own. It is an important position no matter how it comes about. *But God* chose Max. He was obedient at fourteen years old. Knowing how much of a challenge it would be to fulfill that duty, he said yes to God.

I showed Bryan the text. His words: "That's a hard life." At first, I thought he was thinking that it was something Max had chosen, or maybe he didn't believe God had really called our son to preach. Later, I realized that Bryan knew what a difficult road it could end up being, and he was thinking ahead.

He's always thinking ahead. That's why we are good together. I go with what I feel in the moment, he goes with what he feels could be in the future. We are a good team in that way.

That whole day was odd. Earlier, one of Mattie's friends was having some family problems and asked if she could come home with us that morning. I love her friend like one of my own. The normal Lori Grant would say, "Sure, you can stay as long as you need." Yet for some reason that day, there was not one ounce of me that was thinking I should say yes. I have never said no to anyone in need, but God took over my body or something and didn't allow me to feel any kind of empathy in the moment that I was asked if she could come with us. It killed me to say no to her. Totally not me at all, and I was so confused about why I wasn't more like my normal self, but there was not an ounce of my body willing to say yes.

As soon as Max texted me about his preacher calling, I totally understood why I couldn't take her in that day. God knew that I needed to be free from distractions. He needed me to focus on Max, because He knew Max was going to tell me his calling. Isn't that crazy?

Around 9:00 a.m. on Monday, June 18, 2018, when I told her no, God had taken my heart and in an instant changed it from just a mom to a you-better-get-ready-to-be-a-preacher's-mom mom, and I had no idea anything was even going on. *But God* did. He knew exactly what He was doing.

After I read the text and showed Bryan, I headed out to find Max among the two hundred youth at our VBS. I finally found him on the porch with the Bethel Boys talking about what they were going to bring to Colorado. His eyes met mine. I teared up. He looked at me with a *Well, what do you think?* Look, and before I could answer, cousin Brendan started talking to me. I nodded, laughed, fought back tears, and moved on. It was definitely not the time to talk about Max's news. It was hard to talk at all, honestly.

I finally rounded up my bunch that had come to church with us, and we headed home. Once at home, I told Max we needed to talk after his shower. In the meantime, I sat on the couch and "watched" television. I have no idea what was on; I just prayed the whole time that God would give me the right words to encourage and support Max.

So, when he came out from the shower, he sat down by me on the couch. Just the two of us. I can't even really remember how the conversation got started, but I think it was something like me saying, "Are you sure?"

He replied, "Yes, Mama, I'm sure," in a tone like he wasn't stupid and knew when God was calling him to preach.

I tried to get some details out of him. There wasn't much to tell. He said he'd known since July 2017 during revival, when a preacher had preached about finding one's purpose. He said it was then that God revealed what his purpose was going to be. I again said, "Are you sure? How do you know?"

His response: "I just know, Mama. Yes, I'm sure."

I asked him if God had sent him any signs to confirm it. He said he had had lots of signs. He knew it was what he was supposed to do. He said he just didn't want people to think he was crazy or stupid. That's why he hadn't said anything sooner.

Y'all, Max was fourteen years old. Those are big shoes that God had put on him! Since I have never been in shoes quite like that, it was hard for me to guide him from that point. I just told Max that God would always send him signs and speak to him when He had something He wanted Max to do. I told him we were there for him and would drive him wherever God led him to share messages. It was a pretty simple conversation about something so life-altering (or ALTARing), but when God is in charge, the best thing you can do is remove as much of yourself as you can and let Him take over. So, that is what we did.

Max went to his bedroom after our couch conversation, and almost immediately, he yelled for me to come to his room. He *had* to show me what was on TV when he turned it on. It was *Evan Almighty*, a movie about a man, based on Noah, whom God instructs to build an ark when no rain is in sight. Everyone thinks Evan is crazy. Thankfully, we have the Noah of the Bible to look back on and give good examples of how obedience to God pays off in the long run, even when people think you are crazy.

I was so happy to see a sign from God immediately after I talked with Max about signs. I had prayed for the right words to say to him, and God confirmed I had hit the nail on the head and confirmed to Max that although people may think he's crazy, they will see in the end—all in one click of the TV remote and an old movie. Crazy how God works in your life when you are walking close to Him!

I left it all up to Max about who he told and how he told them. He asked me to tell Bryan and Mattie. I told him I had shown Bryan the text. I think it hurt Bryan's feelings that Max hadn't come to him or sent him a text himself. It takes Bryan a long time to ponder things and evaluate the best way to approach every single situation in his life. He looks at things from every angle. It really is helpful most of the time, but I had a feeling that God wasn't going to allow much time for this slow process of pondering that Bryan was used to with everything else. He pondered for long periods of time on projects like dirt-bike fixing and house building.

Max was worried that Bryan was going to be hurt, since he had worked so hard helping Max's racing career get started. Bryan had spent countless hours in the shop prepping Max's bikes and making sure Max had the best of everything: bike, gear, helmet, etc. Max knew his life was about to be changed, refocused. He was worried Bryan wouldn't be happy with his decision to follow God instead of the racing circuit. Max always worries about how other people feel. He has always been that way. *But God* was already weaning Max off of racing. The vomiting was impacting his ability to race.

I did tell Mattie that night. She was still mad at me for not letting her friend come with us. I told her Max's news and tried to help her understand that somehow this was all a part of God's plan and her friend was going to be fine. I could feel that God was working on her friend's situation, too. I told her we had to start focusing on Max now. Mattie would end up being one of Max's biggest supporters.

So, VBS continued through Friday. It was so hard to not say something about Max's preacher calling to someone. That's huge news! But, it wasn't my story to tell, so I had to wait on him to start sharing.

I can't really explain how I felt about it. I was so proud and felt so unworthy of God giving Max and Mattie to me as a parent already. Now having a son chosen by God to spread His word was so overwhelming . . . in a good way. I was pretty much walking around in a fog. I hadn't been in such a fog since God pulled our first church camp together for us effortlessly. When we got the go-ahead four years ago from the deacons to let us organize a church camp, it came together in just a few weeks and was an *amazing* weekend. I was in a total fog for several months over that one. God was just amazing. I did nothing, and He made everything fall into place.

God even made a thick fog fall over the campground where we held our first church camp. Everyone was talking about it. It was beautiful. It had rained all weekend, but ended in a beautiful, thick white fog over the entire campground. Looking back, I guess that could have foreshadowed the thick fog I have been in on and off since that weekend. I think that church camp became a turning point in my life, where I would see that I can take leaps of faith and really surrender everything to God so He can take care of me. It wasn't until writing this book that I realized the significance of that unforgettable fog that weekend.

The Wednesday night of our VBS could not have gone more perfectly. As it turns out, God had a hand in the way our lessons would go. Michael Garrett, a twenty-something-year-old newly-wed preacher, was to give the message to our teens that night. He had preached at our church a few weeks before, and Andy and I both felt led to have him come teach the lesson for us one night. Originally, he was supposed to come on Monday night, but his work schedule only allowed for him to come on Wednesday. Andy and I are flexible, so Wednesday it was.

Bryan, Max, Mattie, and I were the only ones who knew of Max's preacher calling at that point. It wasn't until Michael began giving his testimony that I realized the significance of having him on my heart to come teach our class. At some point in his message, he began talking about his journey as a preacher. He spoke about God calling him to preach as a fourteen-year-old boy.

Wait . . . what?

I had totally forgotten how young he was when God called him to preach! I was thinking he had been a few years older. So, the fact that we had gotten someone with such a similar story to Max's to come teach our kids could only mean one thing: we were on the right track and had who God wanted us to get.

His message was so perfect for Max. He talked about how hard it was as a teenager to have a calling like he did, but still have friends. He told some stories of a few events that happened during his teen years when he had to choose between God and friends, but the bottom line was you can still be a teenager and do fun teenager things without having to sacrifice your promise to God. Hearing his perspective and experience was so good for me as Max's mom. And, it was really good for Max.

Michael went on to say that God wouldn't take away the things you love if you choose to follow Him, like hobbies. He talked about how God can incorporate your hobbies into your purpose if you choose to be obedient and fulfill the purpose He has for you.

Wow. I knew my fourteen-year-old little preacher really needed to hear that. Later on, Max would tell me that Michael's message really helped him a lot.

Some of the Bethel Boys were set to fly out on Friday morning. Tracey has his own plane and flies out of Elliott's airport, a small, private airport through the woods from us. Max was fortunate enough to get to fly with them. What none of them knew, though, was they were flying with a preacher. Our preacher, Jason, was in charge of getting the rest of the group out to Colorado on Saturday on a commercial flight. So, I sent my baby boy, who had just told his preacher calling that no one knew about, on a little ten-seater jet plane out to Colorado for a week, just knowing he was going to be throwing up the whole time and trying to deal with the preacher calling all at the same time . . . alone . . . without me. I had always been able to be there for him for everything. But for this, I had to solely rely on God to take care of him. Although I knew he was in good hands with everyone going out there, it was hard.

Out at Tracey's place in Colorado, they don't have great phone service or Wi-Fi. Not only did Max have a lot going on, but he was in a different state with no way of talking to me. It made this mama's nerves so much worse. I just had to give it over to God. There was nothing I could do for my baby if he was sick or worried about his preacher calling. Nothing. That is a very helpless place to be in. Little did I know that this helpless feeling didn't hold a candle to the helpless feeling I would have in a few months when we would find out about the tumor.

I heard from Max on Saturday. They had gone into town to pick up the preacher and the other Bethel Boys. He was homesick already, bless him. He was having fun, though.

It wasn't until Tuesday that we were able to hear from him again. Tracey did call his wife, Lisa, who sent a message to me letting me know that Max had not thrown up once since he was in Colorado. He was eating and felt great, Tracey said. I couldn't believe it. What in the world? That rarely happened on one day, much less four in a row.

So, when I talked to Max on Tuesday, I was dying to know if he had shared his preacher news with anyone out there. He said he had told the group on Sunday. He said it felt good to tell them. In the back of my mind, I wondered if the preacher calling was what had had his stomach all messed up for the past year.

He called again on Thursday. When he talked to me, he was shopping and trying to figure out what to buy all of us from a store in the town near where they were staying. Not much excitement in our conversation at all. It mainly consisted of listening to him run around the store with Brendan. But, the conversation he had later that night when he called Mattie was way more exciting. He had preached! My fourteen-year-old preacher son had preached his first message in Colorado on a church trip. Wow!

You might think I would've been upset over not getting to hear it. Not at all. God had already prepared me that I wasn't going to be able to be there for Max through this in the way I was used to being there for my kids. I never miss firsts. Never. This was the first "first" that I had ever missed in either of my children's lives. And, I know that it is exactly how God wanted it, and I am okay with that.

We found out later how he told them about his preacher calling. Jason had led a devotion Sunday night. At the end, he asked if anyone had anything they wanted to say. Max stood up and told them God had called him to preach. Bless his little heart. I knew it was going to be sooner rather than later. Jason later told me that he already knew about it. God had prepared him for Max's news, also. The last thing I remember Jason saying at the last night of our VBS, during which Max was already in Colorado, was that he couldn't tell some of the things God had revealed to him, but there were big things coming, and they weren't his story to tell. At that time, I wondered if he knew about Max. He did, but not because Max, me, Bryan, or Mattie told him. God did. It's just crazy how God works.

I had to ask Jason what Max preached about. Max would only tell me "Genesis," and that's about all I got out of him. Jason said Max started out with, "Well, I didn't know where to start, so I figured that I'd better start in the beginning." He said he read a few verses in Genesis that talked about the beauty of God's creations and compared it to the beauty of the Colorado mountains. He told me that Max said, "As God created Adam for a purpose, God wants us, too." He said he gave his testimony and told about his preacher calling. He said Max told them he couldn't spend an entire week with them in Colorado and not tell them about God's purpose for his life. He said it was a "heartfelt and spirit-filled" message. He said that Max continued saying, "God wants us, too," throughout his message. "God doesn't just need the people in the Bible to serve purpose. He wants us, too."

Wow. The wisdom of God shared through a fourteen-year-old.

As soon as Max got back off the plane from Colorado, we ran by the house and grabbed his things for the beach and headed for our yearly two-week vacation in Mexico Beach, Florida. The first week, the week of July 4, we always stay with Ashley, one of my best friends, and her husband, who is Bryan's cousin Johnny. Bryan's other cousin Amy and her family, Lanier, Brendan, and Bailey, also go with us. We've been going on this trip with these people for the last four or five years. Ashley's mom owns the beach house we stay in. But, Bryan, Johnny, Ashley, and I have been going to this house in Mexico Beach for twenty years. That's a whole other book in itself, but this beach and beach house are so special to us.

The second week at Mexico Beach was spent with my family. We've been doing this trip for the last five or six years, as well. We stayed about a mile down the road from Ashley's house in a beautiful home between the pier and the marina. It was so nice to watch the boats coming in and out every morning and afternoon. I thought to myself, *This is the life.* I could live at the beach. We say that every year. Bryan, the kids, and I have been wanting to live at the beach forever. We always sit and think of ways we could end up living at the beach. Little did I know, I would be living at the beach very soon for a period of time.

For two weeks we were going to be with our closest friends and family, so I had to let them know they were vacationing with a preacher. I was so worried that one of the Bethel Boys would tell their parents, and our family and friends would hear the news from someone besides us.

No one made a big deal about it. We all just let Max be Max. There were times when he was quiet and distant, and we just let him be. I wanted so badly to ask him tons of questions, but I didn't. I had to let him and God have their moments.

There were several times throughout that week I would catch Max sitting on the couch near the television. Not watching what was on, but instead on his phone. Apparently this was his escape when he was trying not to think about his duties God had put on him. A few times I stood in the kitchen where I could see him over the mounds of cereal boxes, chip bags, and other snacks on the counter, but he wouldn't notice me. I would think about how I really hoped God had been sending him signs for his messages and his journey of faith he was going to be on soon. It also made me wonder if God was sure he had given a preacher for a son to the right people. I knew I didn't feel worthy of raising someone who was going to spread God's word to others. I knew Max could do it, but I needed confirmation that this was really what he was supposed to be doing and really something that we, as parents, could help him do without getting in the way.

Well, several times God sent me a sign as Max sat on that couch in front of the TV. Several times I would change my focus from him to the TV, and in the bottom-right corner of the screen where you see previews for other shows coming on, I got my confirmation. The show was called *Preacher*. My son was on the right track, and we were raising a preacher. Again, God was in total control. Coincidence? No way. I have had so many "coincidences" throughout this journey that they are no longer seen that way. God is confirming through signs every . . . single . . . day.

We got back from the beach on a Saturday. It was the day before our revival started. Liberty Baptist Church, a church that would soon be as good to us as our own, was in revival, so Mattie and I went to the night service.

We almost didn't go, because neither Max nor Bryan wanted

to. Mattie and I wanted to go, but we were tired and knew that our upcoming week of revival was going to be even more tiring. But, we went anyway. I was blown away by the message.

Remember when I told you about when Max revealed to me he was going to be a preacher for the first time? *Evan Almighty* had been on TV that night. Well, the preacher's message at Liberty Baptist was about Noah. At first when he started preaching and talking about Noah, I thought to myself, *Well, that's a coincidence.* But, as he continued preaching, he spoke mostly about one word in the scripture. He read Genesis 7:16 and talked about how God Himself shut Noah in the ark. I had never thought about how the ark got shut or where God was. I guess in my mind, God told Noah to build the ark. Noah did, then he gathered his family and put them in the ark. The animals went in two by two. They were all on there together, and it rained a lot, which wiped out all the other people left behind. That's about all that I'd really ever thought about. I did think about Noah's obedience and how people thought Noah was crazy until it started to rain.

> *And they that went in, went in male and female of all flesh, as God had commanded him: and the Lord shut him in.*
>
> —Genesis 7:16

God shut him in. God shut . . . him . . . in. God was right there with Noah. He never left him. That's what the preacher was preaching about. God sent Noah on this journey of building the ark, and God stayed with him and saw it through with him. Many times, someone in a leadership position will tell you how they want something done, and then they leave you to do it alone. *But God* stayed with Noah. He sealed him in the ark.

I had never in my life thought about it that way. I felt like I was supposed to hear that message. God wanted me to know that He was going to be right there with Max and us on this journey He had for Max. I needed that message so much. It stuck with me, and I still think about it.

The next day was Sunday, and the first time Max went to our church for a service since he had told his preacher calling in Colorado. It was a big day. He knew he had to tell the news in front of the church. He was nervous, but smiling.

In the parking lot walking into the church, I told him that the preachers have to sit in the front. That's how it has always been. He looked terrified. He asked me if he had to. I told him I wasn't going to make him, but Jason probably would. As soon as we got in the church, Max went to sit with Brendan about three rows back from the altar.

I haven't said this before, but having your cousin for a best friend is pretty awesome. My cousin Travis was my best friend growing up, so I know all about the awesomeness.

So, there sat our preacher son with his best friend. We ended up having to sit at the front of the church in one of the old Sunday school rooms. When the church is full, like it always is for revival, they open those rooms up. When you sit in the old Sunday school rooms, you are facing the congregation. Not only can everyone see you coming in late; you have to face them the whole service.

On that day, I also had a great view of Tracey's son, Jake, and his cousin Caleb. I was so glad they were there. Max had talked a lot about them after he got back from Colorado. They took him under their wings. They had actually been the ones who searched all over the Colorado town they were near to get Max a Bible. It was so important to them to get him a Bible from their trip to Colorado. They had to get in touch with a preacher's wife, and she hooked them up. They even got his name engraved on the front of it! Everyone that was there in Colorado signed it on the inside. It was the best gift, so thoughtful.

I had wanted to see Jake and Caleb so I could hug their necks for going out of their way to show their love and support of my baby boy. They will never know how much that meant to us. All of the people in Colorado will forever mean so much to us, because they supported our baby when we weren't around. Seeing Jake and Caleb's faces when Jason got Max up in the front of the church to tell the church what God had called him to do will forever be one of my favorite memories. They were both beaming from ear to ear like proud parents.

Jason had everyone shake Max's hand. Meanwhile, Jason took that time to come talk to Bryan and me. He told us that Max would be preaching the upcoming youth service Friday night of our revival. He also told us that starting in the next several weeks, he wanted to take Max to some other churches during their revivals on Wednesday nights. He said, "Get ready for your phone to start ringing."

We wanted so badly to be able to take some of this on for Max, but we knew there was nothing we could do. God had called Max, not us, to spread His word. And I was right: Jason made Max sit with the preachers after everyone was finished shaking his hand.

For the rest of the week, we went to the 11:00 a.m. service and the 7:30 p.m. service at revival. Max sat with the preachers each time. I hadn't realized the most recent time he sat with me in church would be the last time he sat with me in church. I honestly don't even remember when it was. He had been racing so much, we really hadn't been at church very much the last year.

It was so hard for me to see him sitting at the front of the church all by himself. The only time he wasn't by himself was when a visiting preacher came. They would sit with him. I tried to sit as close as I could to him. I wanted to feel like I was there for him as much as I could be.

Then, it hit me. The message about Noah kept rolling in my head. Finally, I knew why. He wasn't sitting by himself. God was with him. He will never be by himself. That's hard for a mama to comprehend, but it finally brought me some comfort in the fact that I had to let him go. I was letting him go to God. Those are the best hands to be in. Even so, I still try to sit as close to him as I can get when we go to church, and I just imagine God sitting beside him.

Friday finally got there. Max had been in the best mood that day. I was going to leave him at home to work on his message while Mattie and I went shopping. I thought he might need some time to himself. Surprisingly, he wanted to go with us. I asked him if he was ready for the service. He said he was. He said, "Mama, I think I'm just supposed to tell my story."

I had hoped that would be what he was going to do. I really didn't know the story myself. I knew I had seen the changes in him friendship-wise. He had distanced himself from so many friendships. I knew he was super focused on racing. I knew he was not concerned that he was missing church because of racing. That's about all I knew. So, for him to tell his story that everyone was waiting to hear made it that much more exciting.

The next big question was how many people would hear this message. Usually when there's a new preacher in the area, it is a big deal. Lots of people come to hear them, especially if they are young. We really didn't know what to expect, though.

We had told his racing buddies about his preacher calling and that he was going to preach that night. Several of them came. Their parents came, too. Some met at our house so they could ride with us. Everyone was calling and texting wanting to sit with us. I hadn't promised anyone I would save them a seat. Judging by the calls and texts, I would've had to save the whole front half of the church!

When we first pulled up at the church, this fog came over me. I can't imagine how Max was feeling. It was kind of like an out-of-body experience. I felt like I was floating. My sister, brother-in-law, and niece were the first people I remember seeing in the parking lot. As they approached us, I felt just *blank* inside. I didn't want anyone to talk to me, because I wasn't sure I could formulate words.

I just really can't put into words how I felt as a mom hearing my son preach for the very first time. I just can't. It was surreal. At the same time, I felt very overwhelmed for him. I can't even imagine the pressure he was feeling.

My sister came in clutch with a giant pack of individually wrapped tissue packs, the little ones that you put in your purse. She said she thought we might need them. As usual, she was way more prepared than me. I hadn't even thought of that. She and my mom are always way overprepared. I'm more of a fly-by-the-seat-of-my-pants, let's-just-wing-it kind of person. Thank God He put them in my life! I was definitely going to need those tissues. I don't even know if I thanked her. In that moment, I had no idea how many more times she would be bringing me things I had no idea I even needed in the not-so-distant future.

As people started coming in, the church began to fill up. Before long, the entire church was packed. There was standing room only. The men of the church brought in chairs from the fellowship hall, but there still was no more room for seating. People were having to sit in the hallway that led to the bathrooms. There were so many people there, I was even nervous. The more people that came in the room, the more nervous I got for Max. I'm not even sure "nervous" is the right word, really. I don't know that I was nervous as much as in awe—so in awe of how God was working in our lives that I was in a fog. I couldn't really even concentrate on what was happening around us. People were coming to talk to us, and I'm sure I responded, but I can't remember who they were or what they said.

The more people who came in, the hotter it became in the church. They eventually had to open the doors that led outside in order to get some air circulating. But, the only thing I was concerned with was being able to see Max, and I really wanted to be able to see Jake. I know that is crazy, but Jake's smile the day Max told his preacher calling lit up the room for me. It was already a happy day, but to see someone else beam with joy and pride over something your child has done, well, it's indescribable. So, I wanted to be able to see Jake's face and Max's face. Jake always sat on the front row on the right side as you come in, so we sat on the left side in the deacon section. That's the section where the pews are turned a different way. They face the center of the church instead of the altar. I would be able to see Jake's face from there.

Mattie was asked to sing that night. She would sing before Max preached. She had asked Brea, a family friend who is also like family, to sing with her. They sang "Lord, I Need You" by Matt Maher. I love that song. I had asked Mattie to learn it a year or so before that. The girls went to the back Sunday school room that Mattie and I had decorated the summer before to practice. We had found a wall sign that said "Every Hour I Need Thee" on it. As they were practicing their song, they looked up and saw that sign. It was a God moment for them. They came out talking about it. I had no idea how many times in the next months to come I would think about that moment when they told me about seeing that sign as they were singing. They did a beautiful job, as usual. They sing so well together. And, of course, I cried.

After all the singers sang, it was time for my baby to preach his first message. Bless his heart. He did such a great job. Everyone was so moved by his message. It was so raw and pure. He basically talked about how he had used racing to run from his preacher calling. He said he had known since revival 2017 that God wanted him to be a preacher, and that he had gotten his daddy to take him to every race they could find to help him avoid coming to church. He wasn't just running from his calling; he was racing to get away from it.

He then talked about how he finally decided that he had to do what God wanted him to do. He referenced another message from Liberty Baptist Church he had heard a while back. Preacher Dennis had said, "If God leads you to it, he'll bring you through it." Words of wisdom from Dennis, and now Max. It was the sweetest little message I've ever heard. I just sat and cried through most of it. I couldn't get over the fact that God gave Max and Mattie to us. He trusted us with raising one of His messengers and one of His most beautiful singers. Let that sink in for a minute. I'm still trying to process it. And, one of the best parts of that day was when I saw our preacher's tie. Mattie pointed it out. It was Noah's ark.

We were totally prepared for our phone to start ringing with people wanting Max to come preach at their church. Jason had prepared us for it, and other people had mentioned it. But to our surprise, there were no calls. Not one call right away.

Finally, Tony Holtzclaw from Harmony Baptist Church, my daddy's side's home church, called and asked Max to preach at their youth Sunday service on September 30, 2018, two months away. It gave Max lots of time to prepare. This was good. Maybe God was going to let him ease into it. I was so thankful for that.

Our life the way we knew it was about to change. School was about to start. We had no idea how God was going to get Max through that. Kids can be two ways during something like receiving a preacher calling. They can be supportive, or they can be cruel. I prayed so hard that God was going to take over and make this fourteen-year-old preacher's life smooth. God's way of doing things and my way of doing things are completely different. God is good at what He does, but that's hard to remember sometimes when His plan is so off-the-chart different from how you see things going in your mind.

Our church camp would be the next time Max would preach. It was August 3–5, 2018. The theme was about planting seeds. That seemed fitting for Max. He had been getting so many signs from God in the last year about his preacher calling. So many seeds had been planted in him.

Jason asked Max to preach the Saturday night service, and Max asked me about the verse that went with our theme a few times before we went to church camp. It came from 1 Corinthians 3:6: "I have planted, Apollos watered; but God gave the increase."

For this church camp, the theme came to me pretty soon after our 2017 church camp ended. It came in a vision this time. It was really crazy. I saw the design of the shirt almost flash before my eyes one day. I thought I was losing it, to be honest. I didn't really tell anyone about it. I had a new group planning church camp with me, and they were looking to me for guidance since I had helped with the last three, but I was in no way ready to tell them I was having visions! I had known them all forever, but visions? It really wasn't like that, but really, it kind of was. I can't explain it.

So, I sent them a text saying I thought I knew the theme—

planting seeds—and described the shirt as a watermelon truck. The idea was that all the little (and big) things our church does as outreach (nativity, VBS, etc.) are times that seeds are planted. It was fall 2017 when the theme came to me. I sent the text and pretty much didn't work on church camp again until June 2018.

By this time, Max had been throwing up for over a year, but it didn't stop him from doing all the everyday things. Bryan and Mimi Sue, Bryan's mom, had helped him plant the family garden in early May 2018. Max had wanted to plant watermelon seeds, having no idea that our church-camp theme would incorporate watermelon seeds. Our church-camp-theme plans are always top secret, and that makes some people really mad. I don't care, though. I love surprising people, so that's just one more opportunity for me to surprise a large group of people!

Anyway, they had never planted watermelons before and really had no idea what to expect. When they started growing, Max was so excited! Eventually, there were more and more watermelons. They grew and grew. All of a sudden, he had himself a watermelon patch. It was so awesome to see his excitement when he would come in from the garden every day. When we cut the first one open, the heart was so sweet! It had such a good flavor, but boy, was it seedy. They had more seeds than meat. Max was bummed, but still excited that there were so many. The watermelons were so big, too. They grew long, but not narrowed on the ends. Instead, they grew kind of skinnier in the middle and bigger on the ends. I've never seen a watermelon in stores the shape of his watermelons.

He gave them away to whomever wanted them. It wasn't until we were about to head to church camp that I realized the significance of his watermelon patch. We had a skit that involved watermelons, since our theme was about planting seeds and watermelons are full of seeds. School had just started back, and things were kind of crazy. I was supposed to pick up a watermelon to use, but I forgot. I was so flustered as we were loading the car. I couldn't believe I forgot the one thing that held any real significance to our theme!

As we were going out the door, Max said, "Mama, we can use one of *my* watermelons!"

Now, why hadn't I thought of that? I was so caught up in a perfect church camp that I totally forgot what was going on around my house.

So, we used one of his watermelons to do our skit. The skit involved how every time you bring someone to church, tell your testimony, or bring someone closer to God, you are planting seeds. It was pretty good. Some sweet country cousins at our church did the skit. They talked about their papa and helping him in the garden. They told a really funny story about their papa's first garden lesson when he was younger. He tried to hurry up and plant all the pea seeds for his mom so he could go do the things he wanted to do. Instead of planting one seed per little hole, he put all the seeds in one big hole! Needless to say, they didn't have peas that year.

We all got a laugh out of that, but the lesson you learn from it is so good. In order to get things to grow, you have to plant them correctly. That takes time. You can't have shortcuts or dump it all at once. You have to spread it out, like God intended it to be planted.

The skit finished with the cousins eating and spitting seeds from Max's seedy watermelon at one another. It was cute.

The Saturday morning message about joy from Sam, the other young preacher, was so good. I'm sure Max was dreading having to follow it. He didn't really complain, though. He ran around with all the other kids the rest of the afternoon. I saw him deep in thought at times, but mostly he was fine. He assured me he was ready and prepared for his message, so I left that between him and God.

We all showed up to the conference room dressed in our farmer or gardener attire. We like to dress the theme for the Saturday night service. Seeing what everyone comes decked out in adds some fun and excitement. Max was in his green GNCC racing T-shirt and denim overalls.

Before he preached that night, they asked the youth choir to sing. Max usually loves singing with the youth choir, but this night, his smile went from happy-go-lucky to a face that looked almost sick. I knew what had happened: God had changed his message. The song they sang had a verse that said, "Like a tree planted by the water, I shall not be moved." He was trying not to cry as he sang, bless him. It was time for him to preach right after that, and he looked sick. I felt so sorry for him.

He got up to the podium and apologized for not having scripture to read. He said he had a message that went with our theme prepared, but during the choir song, God gave him something different. Bless his heart for being obedient! He had a sweet little message about standing firm in what you believe and not letting others pull you away from what God tells you. It was about choosing God. He didn't read scripture, but he didn't really need to. The message was so relevant and so perfect. There he was in his overalls, so innocently pouring out the message God had sent. Of course, I cried.

Sometimes at the Saturday night service, we give an opportunity for people to tell others how much they love them or how thankful they are for them. This year, we had packets of watermelon seeds that had "Plant seeds" written on them. The idea was that people could get up and get a packet of seeds, then give it to someone who had planted a seed for God in them.

As Max sat on the front row of the conference center, youth after youth lined up to give him their packet. I couldn't hear what they were telling him, but it definitely was a symbol of support for him. His little pocket was stuffed full of those seed packets! I was so proud of them for being obedient, and so proud of Him for being obedient and giving the message God wanted, not the one he had prepared. It was such a sweet service.

After the service was over, everyone went their separate ways to do whatever activity they wanted. Mattie and the friends she had invited, Avery, Belle, Brea, and Evion, had already headed out. Max and his church buddies had scattered. They had a spoons tournament, hot tubs, bicycles, a pool, volleyball, and several other fun things to choose from. I hung around in the conference center talking to people. When I finally headed for the door, Avery was there. Alone. The other girls weren't with her. She was crying. I sat with her in the conference center and talked to her to see what was wrong. She had a burden for Evion. She had seen Evion crying in the morning service—the one about joy—and was worried that Evion might not be saved.

So, we went to find Evion and the other girls. We saw Max along the way and grabbed him to come with us. I don't know why it feels better to have a preacher around when someone is lost, but it does. Even if he was inexperienced in that area, I grabbed him anyway.

We finally found them in their room in our cabin. I talked to Evion about Avery's concern for her. She said she wasn't sure if she was saved or not, but was willing to go back to the conference center with us to find Jason, our preacher, and get it figured out. She was really calm about it, so I wasn't really sure how this was going to go. Usually, when someone is lost, they are broken-hearted. She seemed sad, but not broken.

Brea, Mattie, Max, Avery, Belle, Evion, and I headed that way. I was so hoping I wasn't going to have to search all over for Jason. Thankfully, he and his wife, Beth, and their daughter Marley were talking to some ladies right outside the conference center. We asked if we could borrow Jason, then we headed into the room where we held our services.

Thankfully, Jason took charge. He had us all grab chairs from the center of the room and circle them together. It looked like a scene in a movie where group therapy is taking place. Marley came to the door to be sure everything was okay, so we invited her into our circle. She and Evion had been on the cross-country team together the year before, so they were friends. Marley had noticed Evion during the joy sermon that morning, also. She was worried about her, too.

We explained to Jason that Evion was confused about her salvation. Evion explained why she was confused, and that led Jason into his message that us Bethel folks had heard many Sundays: "God is not the author of confusion. He will not try to confuse you, but the devil will." He went on to explain how you might feel in your heart when you're lost, and that in order to get to Heaven, you must be saved. "Good works can't get you into Heaven." After his explanation, he left it up to Evion or anyone who felt the need to speak.

Belle gave her testimony. She talked about how she had thought she was saved until she came to our VBS a few years ago. She ended up stopping on the side of the road at her own family church (her papa built it) and praying by herself at the altar.

Evion talked about how the joy message had hit her hard that morning. She had felt like she didn't have the joy she thought she once had. She went on to explain that she felt like she was lost, not saved.

At some point, Jason and the rest of us all got on our knees and prayed with her. I really don't remember what I prayed quietly to myself, other than for God to make it clear to her when she was saved. I don't remember Jason's prayer, but I do remember the sweet smile on Evion's face when she raised her head off the padded chair we were using as an altar. She was saved, she said. It was so sweet.

Evion had had to make a choice that night. She had been invited to a birthday party, but decided to stay with us for the church service instead. She just felt like she needed to be there for Max. I believe God was urging her to stay. Her obedience in coming to church that night led to her salvation. I could not be prouder of that group of kids in that circle that night. They all prayed their hearts out for their friend. Evion was the first person saved at one of our church camps, and it was following two young, brand-new preachers' messages. That should give those boys some confidence to continue to be obedient going forward in their preaching journey.

Chapter Eight

The Laps

But without faith [it is] impossible to please [him]: for he that cometh to God must believe that he is, and [that] he is a rewarder of them that diligently seek him.

—Hebrews 11:6

During a race, each lap is significant. If you have a mishap and crash, if your bike doesn't work correctly, or if you take the wrong line in the woods, you get passed. In order to be the first to the checkered flag, either everything must go pretty smoothly, or you have to work your tail off to get back out in front.

We've seen Max have both kinds of races. The best race I had seen in a long time was when he got a last-place start. He really showed himself that day. His bike didn't start right off the start, and he went into the woods last place. His buddy Levi went into the woods first. He got the holeshot. That's the racing-world term for the first bike to get to the first turn off the start line. There's always a pole with an American flag at this turn signifying the hole shot—the person in the lead off the start. Levi was running great that day; there was nothing stopping him. We were cheering him on, but felt so bad for Max at the same time. As usual, he wasn't feeling well before the race and had done his usual vomiting routine. A last-place start would easily be something to get him down to the point where many in his situation would just give up.

We were timing his laps. He was more than two minutes behind Levi and several others. That's hard to come back from, especially when you have great riders like Levi out in front. But, Max never gave up. He charged each lap like his life depended on it. He put his head down and rode like I've never seen him ride before. With each lap, he closed the gap just a little more. They only had maybe six laps that race, so he was going to have to work harder than he had ever worked in order to catch up with Levi.

Eventually, we noticed he was passing people in front of him and gaining momentum. It was evident that he had a real shot at winning this race. By the fifth lap, he had almost caught Levi. He was so close. We weren't sure he was going to be able to catch him or not, but he was a fighter and was not giving up.

When he came through the woods on the last lap, he was out front. He had passed Levi! Part of me felt so bad for Levi, because he had had such an amazing race, also. He's a few years younger than Max and is such a great kid; you can't help but want to root for him. But, Max out front was probably the highlight of his racing career for me, other than the time he beat a kid named William after they had literally been inches away from one another the entire race. Max had only won that race because William accidentally got off course, and Max realized they were off course before William did. Max turned around and headed the right direction first. Otherwise, I don't think he would've won that one. William is about two years older than Max, so that was an exciting race for us to watch.

So, the fact that Levi had worked so hard to give Max a run for his money was exciting to watch. Racing families are like church families: we all cheer one another on. You can't help it. You want them all to do well. Those are the two races that stand out most in my mind for Max's racing career: the two times he proved that he was a fighter and could ride the wheels off a bike when he wanted. And, he did. He calls it "giving her the berries." I've never understood what the berries are, but am so glad he gave them to "her." He really showed his perseverance and ability to fight in those two races. I have never been so proud of him . . . well, other than the nights he was saved and told his preacher calling. All of those show he's willing to do what he needs to do to come out on top, and he's not afraid to work for it.

We were coming back to school on a church-camp high. It was our first full week back. Max was a preacher, and there was a small buzz about it as people found out. He was still sick, though. After we realized Max had not been throwing up in Colorado, we thought life was going to be good. He had told his preacher calling, and that was what was making him throw up. If only we could've been that lucky.

Shortly after they got back from Colorado, the vomiting started again. With revival and our beach trips, we couldn't get to the doctor right away. We had asked for blood work earlier in the summer and had seen the gastro doctor once we got back. They didn't find anything out of the ordinary. No answers. In our guts, Bryan and I knew something was wrong. Looking back, I know Max did, too.

The Wednesday of that first full week we were back in school, I had to take Max to the doctor. He was so dizzy. The vomiting had been our main concern, but the dizziness was the reason I had taken him to the doctor and gastro over the summer. When I picked him up from the school, the nurse told me she thought he might have some fluid in his ears. Finally, something different. Finally, someone had a possible cause for the symptoms he was experiencing. He seemed to get dizzy in the morning mostly, and he said the dizziness caused the nausea. *Could it be vertigo?* So, off to the doctor we went.

This time we saw the same person who had diagnosed Max's asthma. When he was eight, Max had been on an antibiotic for about three months, thinking the symptoms of his sickness were the result of pneumonia. After we saw that none of the antibiotics were working, I asked the nurse practitioner, Tara Marcus, to check something else. She immediately said it wasn't pneumonia. She diagnosed him with asthma within one short office visit. We had been back three or four times prior to that, and no one else had thought to check him for asthma.

At the practice we use, there are several different doctors and nurse practitioners, so I felt good that it was her we were seeing that day. She looked at his ears, heard the symptoms he'd been experiencing since May 2017, and put him on an antibiotic for an ear infection. She said that might be what had been causing the dizziness, but if he didn't get a lot better fast, she wanted to see him back for a CT scan. I was thinking she wanted to check his ears. That was a Wednesday. At this point, we were still thinking reflux was the cause of the nausea, and now maybe we had the answer for the dizziness.

By that night, he wasn't dizzy and was feeling so much better, so we thought things were about to turn around for him. Thursday he felt great. Friday he felt great. He felt so good, we loaded up and went to Blairsville, Georgia, to a dirt-bike race. This is one of our favorite races of the year. It is probably his favorite of the year, too. Not only is it a mere hour and fifteen minutes away, but it is a cool race. We also know a lot of people in that area. Some of our good racing friends own the property and host the race every year. It is a little bit of a different kind of race than the usual ones through the woods. It is more of a mix of motocross and the woods races. You race in heats, and they combine scores. All of Max's racing buddies would be there. It was going to be so great.

The year before had been a real barn-burner. Literally. Their barn near the sign-up area caught on fire. It was full of hay and fertilizer. Apparently, fertilizer is explosive, so people were scurrying around like crazy trying to remove everything they could out of that burning barn. By the grace of God alone, they did. No one was harmed. It didn't explode. Most of the hay was saved, and the barn was fine. If you had seen the size of the fire coming out of that big barn, you would never have thought anything around it would be still standing, much less the actual barn itself. *But God* is good. There were lots of people praying that day.

We were going into this race thinking that we finally had an answer, and Max was going to race symptom-free. *But God* had other plans.

When Max woke up Saturday morning, he was back to feeling dizzy and nauseous. He was used to the throwing up by now, but the dizziness was starting to get worse. I decided to call Tara Marcus back first thing Monday morning and make an appointment. Something else had to be done.

Max tried to race. The dizziness got worse. He started having heart episodes, and was just sickly. Something was definitely wrong. We ended up loading up and going home early, and it wasn't like him to sick-out. He seemed really worried, too. I could see it in his eyes.

He felt better on Sunday . . . still not 100 percent, but better. I was still planning on calling the doctor the next day. I prayed that God would lead us to the right person on Monday who would end this craziness. I prayed we would get answers. This would be the first of many prayers answered.

On August 13, eight days into the 2018–2019 school year, Max was unable to go to school. He called me that morning and said he just couldn't do it. He was too dizzy. Since I was already at work at the school, I got my classes covered and called the doctor's office as soon as they opened. I only wanted to see Tara again. I wasn't going to settle for anyone else. Finally, we were seeing a doctor who felt like there was more to Max's symptoms than just reflux and an unknown cause of dizziness. She was going to be the one to help us. I could feel it.

Tara was only working at the North Point office. I was fine driving an extra fifteen minutes to see her. As soon as she saw Max, she said we needed to go to the emergency room at Scottish Rite for a CT scan. She seemed really concerned. She was going to call ahead and let them know why we were coming.

So, we headed south to Downtown Atlanta. When we got to Scottish Rite, we did all the normal things you do when you are going to the ER. They checked his weight and blood pressure, and asked us to retell his history about why we were there. Then, we sat in the waiting room. We watched so many people coming in and out. It seemed like some of them might be regulars. I sat there thinking about how blessed we had been, because my kids had always been so healthy. Even with Max's asthma, he never missed school. Mattie was almost never sick. So, I sat there thanking God that this was our first really big scare.

Once we got called back, the ER doctor asked us to explain why we were there. I started with Max's first vomiting episode in May 2017 and ended with Max not feeling like going to school that day. I made sure to tell him we had seen so many people since January, starting with the gastrologist, then cardiologist, having an endoscopy, getting bloodwork done over the summer, and Max being on an antibiotic for an ear infection.

The ER doctor did the same tests all the others had done, and as usual, Max passed all of them. The doctor went on to tell me that he didn't think it was anything big, like a tumor, and a CT scan wasn't really what he would recommend. He said the machine was old and didn't give great information. He thought we needed an MRI. However, the MRI waitlist was so long, he felt like we should go home and schedule the MRI for another day. In my head, I thought I would love to go home, but in my gut, I knew that I needed to push for answers. I thought about Bryan's concerned face on Saturday. I thought about Tara's uneasy expression when she saw us earlier that morning. With my seventeen years of special-education-teacher experience, often dealing with students with severe behaviors, I had learned to read body language, and thinking back to Bryan's and Tara's, I knew if they were there with me, they would push for the CT scan.

So, I did. I asked the ER doctor to help me continue ruling out what Max's symptoms were not, at least. He took Max for a scan, and was back very quickly. Max and I sat to wait on the results, and talked about how we didn't think this doctor believed us, either. Max was starting to get really upset with doctors at this point, except for Tara.

It wasn't long before the ER doctor came back in. He was acting upbeat and had a look on his face that I couldn't really read. He was still smiling and making some kind of clicking noise with his mouth. He then pulled up a chair. I knew when I saw him go for the chair that we were about to get an answer to all of our questions.

I was right. He came right out with it. They had found "something." "Something" was on the scan. It was on the back of Max's head, near his spine area. It took him ten seconds to tell me that we had just entered a parent's worst nightmare.

At the beginning of each of Max's races, Eddie, the race organizer, gives the boys on the line a ten-second warning that he's about to wave the green flag signaling them to start their bikes. This doctor had just taken ten seconds to make us stop in our tracks. I just stared at him blankly, speechless. This would be the first of many times during this journey I was stopped in my tracks. So many things ran through my mind.

"Something"? What is "something"? Is that a tumor? Is it an aneurism? What is "something"? How is Max taking this? I can't look at him. If I look at him, I'll cry. Just keep staring at the doctor. He can't read my face like Max can. Max has always been able to read my face. He will know I'm scared to hear more details. Am I scared? Wait. I'm not really scared. I know God's got this. He wouldn't have called Max to preach if He wasn't going to let him do it more than twice, would he? Why would He call him to preach at fourteen, only to allow whatever this is to kill him? We can do this. God has this. He has always had this. I prayed for answers, and now I'm getting answers. Can I look at Max yet? He's so quiet. I know if he's starting to cry, I will start to cry and be less convincing that we don't need to worry. God has this. I need to say something. I don't know what to say.

I asked the doctor what would happen next. He stared at me for a minute, then, with a blank look on his face, he finally said, "We are admitting him to the hospital. I'll have the neurosurgeon come in soon."

You would think I would've hung onto the word "neurosurgeon," since that is such a big deal, but the word "admitting" is what I was stuck on. I had to process what that meant.

Wait . . . "admitting" means we are staying here. We don't get to go home. I don't have any clean panties in the car. I will need new panties. Max will hate staying here overnight. Max is going to be so upset. I can't look at him yet. I'm not ready to look at him. He's only fourteen. I have to look at him. I know he's terrified. But, if I look at him, I'm going to cry, then he will cry, then we will both lose it. I've been strong so far, and I need to keep that up. I have got to look at him soon, or he is going to worry more.

I looked at my son. He had tears in his eyes. Now, I did, too.

Okay, Lori. You can't lose it now. You've got to be strong. You can't let him get scared. He needs to fight this, and he can't if you fall apart. Your strength will make him strong. You have to say something . . . something that will take that scared look off his face. Something that will make him not worry so much. Something really good. What can you say? What will get to him the most?

Finally, I spoke. The only thing that made sense to say at this moment was, "But God's got this, baby. He wouldn't have called you to preach if he wasn't going to let you. You are going to be okay. I can feel it. It's okay."

We both cried a little, but not like you would think. Just a few tears rolled down our cheeks. I hugged him so tightly. I hugged him like hugging him was going to protect him from this "thing" in his head. But, it was on the inside. I couldn't put a bandage on it, or ice it down and make it better. *But God* could make it better.

I looked back at the doctor, who still had that blank look on his face. He didn't really know what to say, either. I explained that Max had just told his preacher calling, and he was going to be fine because God needed him to preach.

As it turned out, this doctor was from Jasper, Georgia, which is only about twenty minutes from our house. He finally said something that made sense, asking, "Can I pray with you?"

That's when the waterworks started pouring out. I had held it together pretty well, I thought, until that moment. *But God* was letting me know He was in this thing with us.

The doctor grabbed both our hands, and he prayed. I honestly have no idea what he prayed. I was still trying to figure out what was even happening.

Over a year of searching for answers, and God finally sends them after *Max tells his preacher calling? What is even going on? Am I dreaming? Is this really happening?*

This was the first of many times I found myself asking those questions. It was also a time I felt complete peace—a peace that I will never be able to explain; a peace that took my feet and walked for me; a peace that took my mouth and talked for me; a peace that gave me a strength that I had never felt before. I was like Popeye right after he ate a can of spinach, only it was spiritual strength causing the physical strength. I had spiritual spinach straight from the grocery store of God. It made absolutely no sense in the scenario we were in that I would have peace, but I had peace. Because of God.

I honestly can't tell you much about the order of things from that point on. It was all a blur. The hospital minister, Bonnie, and a child-life specialist came in and prayed with us. At that point, I was getting the message loud and clear that God was with us. I think we may have met Jen, the neurosurgeon's assistant. Then, before I knew it, Max was in a wheelchair and we were headed from the ER to the first-floor neuro unit to be checked into a room.

I must've floated from the ER to room 114. I have no idea what even happened between the two. I am sure we went in an elevator or through some doors. I honestly can't tell you. I do remember that when we rounded the nurses' station, they asked the person pushing Max if we were headed to room 119. She said we were. The person at the desk told her to take us to 114. That meant nothing to me. I had no clue where I even was.

The person pushing Max turned and told me we got a room upgrade to "the big room." She was super excited about it. It wasn't until I ventured out in the next few days and looked at the other rooms that I realized we really did get lucky. Room 114 made two, if not three of the other rooms. They didn't know it, *but God* knew we would end up needing that big room eventually.

Once we got in there and were alone for a few minutes, Max and I finally broke down a little. I told him this thing was bigger than us, *but God* was going to get us through. He asked me if he was going to die. How I held it together with my fourteen-year-old asking if he was going to die is totally an act of God, but I held it together and answered him. I told him he was going to live, because God would not have called him to preach if He wasn't going to let him do it. I told him this was part of God's plan, and we both had to fully trust in Him in order to make it through. I told him to pray and believe that God could heal him, and He would, but that it wasn't something I could do for him. Just like when he asked God to save him when he was nine, this had to come from him, not me. He said he could do that, and he did.

At some point in the ER, I called Bryan to let him know what was going on. On the phone, we decided that it was probably best that we wait until we knew what we were dealing with for sure before we let people know what was going on. Bryan planned on heading to the hospital to join us as soon as he got off work. We knew that could be anywhere between 5:00 p.m. and 9:00 p.m., so I wasn't expecting him anytime soon.

The hospital still planned on doing an MRI that afternoon, hoping they could squeeze Max in that day. They wouldn't let him eat, because he had to have an empty stomach for the MRI. We were both starving. Then, they told us they couldn't get to the MRI that day, and we could finally eat.

It hit me that Max was supposed to go with Jason, our preacher, to start visiting revivals on Wednesday. I still had no idea what we were dealing with, but I felt pretty sure Max wasn't going to make it for his first visit. I sent Jason a text that had very basic information, including all I knew at that point, and as I sent it to him, something told me I needed to start asking for prayer. I knew we couldn't do this thing alone. Bryan would be mad that I hadn't waited to tell people like we had talked about, but he would get over it.

So, I asked for prayer from the church—something I almost never do for us. I ask for other people, but not for us. But, I knew this thing was going to be bigger than us. I sent the text to a few of our family members and closest friends, and asked for best-case-scenario prayers. The tumor was there. Nothing I could do about that, but I could ask that they pray for God to give us the best-case scenario, and they did . . . and He did.

Suddenly, I realized I hadn't told Mattie. How in the world was I going to try to get the words out over the phone with her and still sound strong?

I really can't remember much about the conversation. I remember silence. I remember wanting to snap my fingers and be there at home with her so I could hug her, too. I remember thinking how life-changing this whole thing was that I was having to tell my almost-sixteen-year-old daughter that her baby brother was about to be in for the fight of his life, and we would need her to bring us some underwear. All we had with us were the clothes on our backs, and we had no idea how long we would be in the hospital. I told her I would text her a list of things to bring us.

Bless her heart, her friend Payton had brought her home for me once I realized we weren't going to be back in time to get her from school. I had basically abandoned her. Thankfully, she had told her friends Jenna, Evion, and Avery, and they sprang into action. They were at our house immediately and were so sweet to stay with her.

From that point on, our phones never stopped ringing and

texts never stopped coming through. Some people wanted to come visit. Some wanted to let us know they were praying. Some wanted to bring food, or feed our dogs, or cut our grass. I have no idea how everyone knew so fast, but the whole town knew immediately. I had no idea how much we were loved by our little community until that day.

By the time Bryan made it to the hospital, we already had that big room full of people. We had our meltdown together in the hallway, and then found ourselves a quiet spot to sit in the family waiting room nearby. He wasn't happy that people were there before he was and that I had told people about the tumor. But, I hadn't been sure when Bryan would get off work, and we needed people. Max and I aren't really the let's-deal-with-this-on-our-own kind of people that Bryan and Mattie are. We need people to hug us, talk to us, and make us laugh. We just need people.

Boy, did we have them. One thing I wanted to be sure, though, was that the people who came were upbeat and positive. Max reads people so well, and I knew if he saw anyone break down and cry, he would break down and cry.

One of my best friends, Kim, was the first one down there. She stopped and got Max supper. Kim is such a positive person. I make fun of her all the time, because you don't see her cry very often. I was so glad she was there. She made us both laugh, and helped pass the time until some other people came.

I honestly don't know who came next. My mom, dad, sister, and brother came at some point. The Youngs came, Rob and Tracy. Their daughter, Avery, and Mattie have been friends since kindergarten. Bryan's mom and sister came. Our preacher, his wife, their son, and another friend from church, Chris, came. Chris's mom, Deedra, had a brain tumor several years ago. She and I were working together at the time. We had so much fun together. I was with her the day she found out about her tumor. I think of her almost every day now that we have gone through this. She has her own tumor journey to tell and is still an inspiration to us all to this day. She was only concerned with getting better so she could see her boys grow up, and God let her do that! She had a few complications, but she hasn't let the effects of her tumor hold her back at all. I really thought of her mom the most throughout our journey. She was strong for her daughter, and I was trying so hard to be strong for my son.

We were so blessed with so many family and friends that night and throughout the duration of our stay at Scottish Rite. The first day was already such a blur. Something told me to start writing down the visits we had and the gifts they brought. I made a list after Bryan and Mattie left to go home. They were the last to leave. That was a tearful moment. Actually, every time they left was a tearful moment. Max and I would sit and cry, wondering how we were going to try to find joy in this journey.

What did God have in store for us? We were certain there was a reason all of this was happening. We curled up in his bed that first night and prayed. Then, I played my Jesus playlist as we tried to drift off to sleep. You don't get much sleep typically in the hospital, but we were able to sneak a few hours in, thankfully.

Bright and early Tuesday morning, we were woken up to go to the MRI at 6:00 a.m. I wasn't sure if doing the MRI that early was a good thing or a bad thing. I felt like it was probably bad, meaning that Max's tumor was a big deal and had to come out.

Unfortunately, Max wasn't able to do the MRI as planned. Of course, he threw up first thing in the morning, and apparently they won't let you get an MRI if you are a "puke risk." He was also a "fall risk," according to the bracelet they put on him. I kind of laughed when they did that. If they had only seen all of his activities over the past year and a half that he had had this tumor, they would've, too. He was a "fall risk" because he might fall going to the bathroom. That was just so funny to me. I try to find humor in all bad situations. That is the Henson way. My dad's side of the family has always been upbeat, rather than dwelling in gloom and doom over the sad things.

The fact that Max had acted so normal was probably why none of the doctors before took us very seriously. I think that was all part of God's plan, though, because if any of those doctors had taken us seriously, we wouldn't have ended up in the hospital on the most amazing, Godsent neurosurgeon's shift, and so many other things wouldn't have happened.

We had so many nurses who had the same name as special people in our lives. Our first nurse was named Ashley. I have an Ashley. Ashley is one of my dearest friends/family. She's also an amazing nurse. She just has such a calming effect on people. It wasn't the same Ashley, but just having the same name as one of my dearest friends was calming to me.

I can't remember all the nurses who had familiar names, but each nurse or tech for the first two or three days had the same first name as someone we knew and loved. I know it seems trivial, but it's the little things that get you through something like this. I felt like God was sending me little signs that He was there the entire time.

After the MRI was finally okayed by the doctor, they ended up having to sedate Max. He tried without sedation, but got dizzy, causing nausea. So, I watched them sedate him as he sat ready to go in the MRI tunnel, and then they sent me for a two-hour "break." Yeah, right. A break. That was funny, too.

I went back to the room they started us out in for the MRI and turned on my Jesus playlist. Then, I cried harder than I've ever cried in my life for at least a solid five minutes.

How did we get here? What is even happening? Is Max going to be okay? Is God really as in this thing as it seems? Am I crazy to think that? So many questions went through my head. *But God* spoke to me immediately. He told me to suck up the tears, because He *did* have this and Max *was* going to be fine. And, just as quickly and heavily as the tears had started, they abruptly stopped.

I've never had anything like that happen. Once I have a breakdown, it's hard to stop crying on a dime like that. I don't have many breakdowns; I am typically very strong. I had the choice to trust God and lean on Him, or be weak and worry constantly. I chose to trust completely.

My thoughts took me to what I had told Max the day before about God calling him to preach and having big plans for him, and how God wasn't going to let this tumor stop that. I couldn't believe the next text I got. It was immediately after that thought came into my head. It was Christy Perry, a former coworker. She said, *God's got this and obviously has huge plans for Max.*

I couldn't believe my eyes as I read the text! She and I never text one another. I was even more convinced that God was all in this thing. Isn't it funny how the people whom God sends your way who you least expect, and with a message that you expect to hear from someone else, are the ones who stand out the most? It just goes to show that when God puts someone on your heart, you better move. Even if you believe they think you are crazy for thinking of them, be obedient. I definitely learned that through this. Obedience is key. The only reason Christy even knew what was going on was because a coworker of hers goes to our church and was reading the prayer request that I had Jason send out. God was all kinds of in this. I almost didn't ask Jason to ask for prayer, but God wouldn't let me not ask. It was just crazy how that little obedience on my part (for myself) would end up with someone else sending me a text that I needed in the very moment that I needed it. I am constantly in awe of the way God works. I always have been, but for sure am now.

After the MRI was over, we were taken back to room 114. The neurosurgeon was supposed to come by with the results. We had met him briefly the night before, but hadn't discussed anything regarding Max's treatment plan yet. Bryan was still at work, so when the neurosurgeon came by, I met with him by myself. I videoed the conversation so I wouldn't forget the details. I am so bad at medical details. I just can't remember all that stuff when doctors talk. I knew everyone would be relying on me to relay the information from the neurosurgeon, and I was still in such a fog.

Before the neurosurgeon came in, I had been so nervous about the results from the MRI. I knew God was using us for something, and this was all a part of His plan, but I had so many different possible outcomes run through my mind. I was trying to trust God's plan, but I felt fearful that His plan was going to lead Max to a life of preaching from a wheelchair or using a Braille bible. I wasn't sure if we were strong enough for those outcomes. In fact, I knew I wasn't. I had been a special-education teacher for seventeen years. I knew how hard life could be, and I knew how blessed we were to have had healthy kids up until this point. I was so afraid that God's plan was going to turn our lives upside down in a way to be a light to others. I wasn't sure I was going to be able to be that light if I didn't get *my* son back in his original state after surgery.

So, the neurosurgeon took me to the nurse's station to show me the MRI results. I watch a lot of medical TV shows, but I had never imagined getting results from my son's MRI while sitting at a busy nurse's station with people walking by. On TV, you always see people getting bad news in a hospital room or a more formal doctor's office. In the strangest way, this setting calmed me. It was like this was not as big of a deal as we were thinking, and we were just going to sit at the nurse's station and chat a bit. I could do this.

I later realized that it wasn't just the setting that calmed me; it was the neurosurgeon. I swear he had this shield of God's Holy Spirit all around him. As long as I was in his (or His) bubble of protection, I was fine.

The neurosurgeon pulled up the MRI results on the computer, and in the most mesmerizing tone of voice, he explained to me the location, size, and depth of my son's brain tumor. Now, you would think seeing something like this would immediately put you on your knees. Nope. I was calm—eerily calm. I videoed the whole conversation. I listened to him tell me that my son had a tumor on his brain stem, and it had to come out on Thursday, two days away. He continued explaining the risks of the location and size of the tumor. He explained that Max could have vision and hearing loss, paralysis, cognitive setbacks, trouble with speech, breathing, and eating. He could end up on a ventilator, feeding tube, and in a wheelchair. He could end up in a coma, and even death was a possibility.

I calmly had a conversation about all of these possible outcomes with this man I had never met before this week, but had complete and total faith in, all because I had such faith in God. I knew that just like Max's first message I had heard him preach, "If God brings you to it, He can bring you through it." I never shed a tear while sitting with the neurosurgeon.

Why am I so calm? What is even happening? I couldn't get these thoughts out of my mind.

I did not tell Max all of the possible outcomes. We were trying to keep him as upbeat as possible. The first day we were there, I had told him we could approach this one of two ways. We could worry about it and stress, or we could leave it in God's hands and surrender it all to Him. This time, we talked about how we could be positive and upbeat, or we could be sad. He and I both decided to be positive and surrender it all to God. I tried to tell him his attitude with everything that happened would affect his outcome in recovery. So, Max decided he wanted to be positive (as much as he could).

We took it day by day. We all did. Bryan, Mattie, Max, and I had to be a positive team and try to find the good in every day of this journey. We made sure to make it known to all who came to visit that we were being positive and not crying about things. I knew enough about sickness to know that the people who give up instead of being positive usually end up in a way worse situation.

Not everyone we were close to was able to keep a positive outlook. I could see it in their faces. They were worried. I had to avoid those people. I was doing good to keep Max, Mattie, Bryan, and myself happy and positive. I couldn't hold up anyone else, and I was not about to let their worry get into our bubble of positivity we were trying to keep afloat.

I was so thankful for the people who could hold us up. They got us through. Their strength strengthened me, so I was able to keep Max positive. Weakness was just not an option, and honestly, it still isn't. I avoid weak people. I don't have the strength to keep my family positive on a brain-tumor journey and deal with those people who are weak for whatever reason. We have a choice to be strong and rely on God, or be weak and worry about everything. I choose strong.

During this journey, so many people were wanting to *do* things for us. I was so thankful we had so many people loving and praying for Max and us. But, there wasn't anything anyone could really *do* besides that. We just needed sources of strength, that's it. God was the only one who could *do* anything for us. All we needed were people to be strong and to pray.

We had an overwhelmingly great number of people visit us at the hospital, specifically on Wednesday night. It was the night before surgery. All the Grant cousins, most of the racing buddies, several great aunts and uncles, all the grandparents, aunts, uncles, and a few friends who are like family came. Max was very solemn that night. He later told me he was terrified. I know he was thinking that this might be the last time we all were together like this. I was.

One of his former baseball coaches, Donnie, and his wife, Lynn, came. Their son was working at the building supply with Bryan at the time. As soon as Donnie came in, I knew he was the person I was supposed to ask to pray with our group of visitors before they all left. I hadn't seen him in forever, so he was probably going to think I was crazy. *But God* wanted me to, so I had to ask him.

Close to the end of visiting hours, we all joined hands in one of the activity rooms, and Donnie prayed. All day long I had thought about how God is the Great Physician. Bryan and I had such a good feeling after meeting the neurosurgeon and hearing his plan, I couldn't imagine Max being in better hands (except God's hands). That is what Donnie prayed. He so strongly prayed that God was the Great Physician and was going to heal our baby.

I totally lost it on the inside. I hadn't told anyone my thoughts that day. God continued to amaze me. He had this! He had continued to show me that He was with us each and every day we were in the hospital.

After everyone left, Mattie, Max, Bryan, and I sat in Max's hospital room. We were all staying the night together. One of the nurses helped us find another couch cushion that wasn't being used so we could all sleep in the same room. It was so important for us to be together one last time . . . just in case it was the last time. None of us spoke of that idea, but I feel sure we were all thinking that it could very well be the last day we were together like "normal."

As we tried to settle down, I looked around the room we had been in for three days. It had stuff everywhere. We had been given so many gift baskets that I hadn't had time to go through most of them. Max's school had sent one that had snacks, cards, and books in it. I searched through it and ran across an envelope with a large, oddly shaped object in it. I had to know what it was, so I opened it first. It was a cross from Israel. It was probably the most beautiful wooden cross I had ever seen. It was the perfect size to put in your pocket. I gave it to Bryan, and he ended up keeping it in his pocket the rest of the time in the hospital.

There was also a book of daily devotions, words of wisdom and faith. Out of curiosity, I flipped it to August 16, surgery day. As soon as I began to read, an overwhelming sense of God's spirit surrounded me. The verse for the day was 2 Chronicles 7:14: "If my people, which are called by my name, shall humble themselves, and pray, and seek my face, and turn from their wicked ways; then will I hear from heaven, and will forgive their sin, and will heal their land." All we had done was pray for the last three days, but God was continuing to amaze me. I didn't feel like I deserved so many moments like that.

A friend of mine whom I used to work with, Natosha, tried to get something to me that day. Her church was going to pray over a handkerchief, and she wanted to get it to Max. At the time she texted me, I didn't really think much about the handkerchief. It was a sweet gesture, but I had so much going on and so many visitors, I didn't really read the whole text. Later, once things settled, I was able to see that she had sent me a picture of the handkerchief. Then, it hit me: I had never bought one for Max to keep in his pocket after he had told his preacher calling. I had gone shopping to get his version of preacher clothes (khaki shorts, a collared button-up shirt, and some nice shoes and belt that matched). That's about as preacher-like as I was going to get him, and God was fine with it. Yes, I actually prayed about what my preacher son should wear. But for some reason, I had not gotten him a handkerchief. He had wiped his tears on his collar the first night I saw him preach at our revival, and I was so embarrassed that I, as his mom, hadn't thought of him needing a handkerchief. I kept forgetting to get him one. I never did. I had actually beat myself up over that at one point the first day we were in the hospital. I was so mad at myself for being so caught up in whatever else was going on in our world that I forgot to take care of Max's preaching needs. *But God* provided what I hadn't. He took care of it. Max's first handkerchief had been prayed over.

You can't get one like that at the outlet mall, that's for sure.

Chapter Nine

The Surgery

And this is the confidence that we have in him, that, if we ask any thing according to his will, he heareth us.

—1 John 5:14

On Thursday morning, the day of surgery, Bryan, Mattie, and I went down to the operating-room area with Max. I had gotten used to the nurses and staff on the first floor, where his room was, so meeting new people was nerve-wracking in this situation. You will not believe the name of the first person we met down there. She was our operating-room intake nurse, and her name was Joy.

I fell apart. Mattie and Bryan looked at me like I was crazy, but I was so overwhelmed by yet another one of God's ways to show me He was all in this thing. I told you the young preacher's message about joy at church camp had stuck with me. The whole time we had been in the hospital, I had tried to find joy in the journey. I was so desperate for signs that God was in this. He had gone and done it again in such an overwhelming way that I just couldn't contain *my joy* anymore. I was crying tears of joy like crazy! Mattie and Max still make fun of me for crying over Joy, the person. I cry every time I try to explain why it was so significant to me, and they continue to make fun. Crazies.

The next person who came in the room was a lady named

Lorie. She was a friend of Lisa Perry, the human-resources officer at the school county office, but also a neighbor whom I had known since high school, when she was a teacher. Lisa had sent her to check on us. Lorie didn't work directly where we were, but nearby, and said she was there if we needed her. I didn't really *need* her, but since she had my name and God was continually sending people with names of people that we knew, we needed her as another confirmation that God was in this.

Judi was the nurse who would be calling us hourly to let us know how surgery was going. Bryan has an aunt named Judy. I took that as another sign. I wish I had written down all the names of people who helped us in the hospital and all the signs God sent. There were so many. I wanted to try to include them all in this book, but honestly, most of the stay at Scottish Rite is a blur.

Judi was going to let us know what number Max counted to when they gave him the anesthesia so he could let his friend Will know. They were in competition. Will had gotten to seven when he had anesthesia for a surgery he had a while back. Max was determined to get past seven. We would later find out from Judi that Max had beat Will. He counted to eight! I think Judi was more excited than we were. It was comforting to know she cared about our son.

The moment came for them to take Max back for surgery. They loaded him up on "happy juice" to calm his nerves before they took him back, so he was all smiles and giggles. We walked alongside his bed as they rolled him to the doors that open into the OR. We took one last picture smiling with him, and then they took my baby to open his skull to operate on a tumor between his brain stem and his cerebellum. Of course, I broke down as soon as those doors closed. Bryan did, too. Even Mattie was tearful, and she's usually stone.

Bryan, Mattie, and I went back to room 114 to wait on the first call from Judi. Max would go to the pediatric ICU (PICU) after surgery, but room 114 was ours until surgery was over. By the time we got back, someone had loaded up all the snacks and gifts friends and family had sent in the three days we had been there. It only took six wagons to load it all up. There was a wagon train outside the door. It was really funny. I went through the wagons and got out the things we needed for PICU, and someone took the rest to our car. I have no idea who did what, but I'm so glad we are so loved and had so many people with us that morning.

Bryan's sister, Kristin, had said the prayer before we headed to the OR that morning. God had put her on my heart that morning. She said the most perfect heartfelt prayer imaginable. Everyone had gathered around Max in his bed, and we all laid hands on him and each other. It's one of the most spiritual moments I've ever been a part of outside an altar call at church.

My sister and mom had been bringing me random things I didn't know I needed until I needed them, like dry shampoo. I didn't know I was out, but they did and hooked me up. Poor Mattie had packed mine and Max's bags. We never came home from the hospital from the ER visit until he was discharged nine days later. I can't imagine how she felt as she was at the house alone packing our things for the first few nights.

The neurosurgeon had told us a few timelines before surgery. He had told us that recovery time could be anywhere from five to eight days. He told us surgery could last anywhere from five to seven hours. He told us the tumor consistency could be anywhere from soft, like Jell-O, to hard, like a baseball. The texts that were going out to the church and friends asked for people to pray for best-case scenario and Jell-O. I found out later on that there was a hashtag #prayforjello going around. Students at my school wore stickers and wrote it on their arms. There were student-led prayers at both the junior high where Max attended school and the high school where I worked and Mattie attended school that morning. Facebook had blown up with prayer requests for Max. People all around the United States were praying for Jell-O. I even had a student texting me that she had someone in Israel praying for him. We had felt all the prayers since day one. Max and I had many conversations about how strongly we had felt the prayers. Today was the day we needed them most.

Those hourly updates crept by. I didn't think that day would ever end.

Bryan and I had to find ourselves a place to be alone as we waited for Judi to call. We loved having all the family, church family, and friends by our side, but the chit chat and small talk were just too much for us. People would ask questions as they popped in their heads. We didn't have answers, and honestly sometimes their questions were too scary to let my mind go to, and that was just too much for us. We didn't want them to leave, but we had to be alone.

We ended up in the most random place. We walked around to the chapel and found a garden outside, but we ended up sitting in the main lobby beside the electrically programmed piano, watching the fish swim around in the tank across the room and all the people pass by. If you have never been to a children's hospital and people-watched, you should try it sometime. Even on your worst day, you have it made compared to some. We sat in silence most of the time, feeling alone. *But God* was with us.

We did wander into the gift shop across the hall from the couch we sat on. As we wandered around talking about things that Mattie and Max would like, we ran across the daily-planner-and-journal section. There was one journal that "spoke" to me. I am a firm believer in things speaking to me. That's how I choose gifts for people, decorate my house, pick out outfits. I wait for things to speak to me most of the time. That may sound crazy, but when I let myself be in a place where I get my thoughts out of the way and wait on things to speak to me, I always end up better off.

So, this one planner spoke to me. It had flamingos on it. I don't even like planners. I've never been able to keep up with them. I've never been that organized. But, this one just wouldn't let me walk away. I bought it. The flamingos were significant to me. I had found a saying a while back that said, "Be a flamingo in a flock of pigeons." I love that. It means that anyone can look just alike and act just alike, but it takes a special person to stand out and look so majestic doing it. To stand out in a good way is to stand out in a Godly way.

To me, both of my kids do that. Neither is easily influenced to do things that they know are not pleasing to God. In a lot of ways, Max was that flamingo in that he wasn't afraid to stand out and set himself apart. That started when God started dealing with him with his preacher calling.

The spring before we found the tumor, Max wore a loud flamingo-pattern jacket to the spring dance, and it was perfect for him. He found it online and told me the only way he would go to the dance was if he could wear that jacket. So, flamingos it was. I made him compromise with me on the pants and tie. A blue jacket with pink flamingos all over it is loud enough. It doesn't require a matching tie and pants, in my opinion, especially if you are on the court for the dance! Max was on the court. He wasn't very excited about that, but Brendan was on court, also, and that was the only way Max was even willingly participating in the first place. Brendan is another flamingo. He is like Max and Mattie in that he is okay not doing what the crowd is doing. He's such an original in such a good way. His little brother, Bailey, is, too. They are all great kids who love Jesus. Apparently their peers think so, too. Brendan and Max both placed on court. I was very proud of both of them.

Bryan and I cried and laughed, but mostly sat and watched people while we waited on the calls from Judi. We waited for that hourly call and would text it to Mattie, my sister, Buffie, and Bryan's sister, Kristin. They would send it out to whomever had asked them to keep them informed.

You would think the phone calls we received were informative. Nope. We would get one sentence about what was happening. The first one, "The doctor has just opened the skull and is examining the specimen," was an image I didn't want to think about. And one of the last ones, "They just brought him back from an MRI and found there was tumor left, so they are going back in," was the most difficult, I think. We did really well up until the one about the MRI. That was the one that got to us. At that point, Max had been in surgery for roughly six hours. We were hoping that at the six-hour mark, he would be back in recovery, almost ready for us to see him. That was not the case. That is the moment we both fell apart.

At some point in the day we talked about how it was funny that the worst day of your life (in our case, the day our son was in brain surgery) could also be the best day of your life (the day our son was healed). God had finally provided us with answers. He had led us to a hospital that gave us those answers. He had given us the surgeon who calmed all of our fears, and today was going to be a good day.

We both fell completely apart in a stairwell trying to get to the Koi pond outside to have a change of scenery. We sat on the steps, and I cried my heart out. Bryan sat with his head in his hands and let me.

As I cried and hyperventilated, some random man who worked at the hospital came up the stairs. He went through the door we had just come through, and he used a badge to unlock the door. At that moment, Bryan jumped up in a panic. He was sure we were locked in the stairwell. Sure enough, the door was locked. My tears stopped and hysterical laughter took over. Our baby was about to be out of surgery, and we were locked in a stairwell. Maybe I have a whacked sense of humor, I'm not sure, but I really needed that laugh in that moment. I felt like we were in a movie for a minute.

Turns out, we weren't actually locked in. The door at the bottom of the steps wasn't locked and led us straight to the Koi pond, where we sat in the sun. There is just something about being by a body of water, even if it's a small Koi pond, that changes your perspective. I laid on a bench with my Jesus music and Bryan sat by the still water. For a moment, time stood still.

We got a message from Judi saying they were closing up and Max would be headed for recovery soon. We knew that he was supposed to be in recovery for about two hours, so we headed back to room 114 to meet Mattie and try to relax for a few minutes before the doctor came.

Once we got in there, we were all alone. I'm not sure where "the people" went. That's what I had called all of the family, friends, and church family that were there that day. I just know that the room was empty, and when Mattie got there, our family would almost be complete.

Mattie's birthday was on Sunday. Max had made it through surgery alive. The condition he was in for the rest of his life was what we were waiting to hear from the neurosurgeon.

Will he be able to help celebrate Mattie's birthday with us on Sunday, or are we in for a rocky rest of his life? Will he be mobile? Will he be able to move both arms and both legs? Will he be able to see us with his eyes? Hear us? Speak to us? Eat? Will he need a ventilator? Feeding tube? Wheelchair? Therapies?

So many questions, and we would have to wait until we saw the doctor to get answers. The doctor may not even be able to answer all of those questions right away. All we knew at that moment was Max was alive and we were scared to death. *But God* had him.

It wasn't very long until the neurosurgeon came into room 114. Bryan, Mattie, and I were just staring into space. Ashley was the only one in there with us at the time, and I asked her to stay when the neurosurgeon came in. She was a nurse, so she understood medical jargon. She could explain any questions I had if the neurosurgeon couldn't make it make sense to me. She could also help pick us up if there was bad news. She was strong. No weakness allowed. We just couldn't handle it. It was all we could do to hold ourselves up in those hours leading up to this moment.

We had Madison, Bryan's cousin, guarding the door outside with instructions not to let *anyone* else in. That was a decision Bryan and I made together. We knew we needed to be free from distractions, worried faces, and chit chat with questions.

The neurosurgeon pulled up a chair when he came into the room. That brought back a sudden wave of awful that reminded me of the ER doctor bearing the news of the tumor only a few days ago. I honestly don't remember what the neurosurgeon said up until the part where he said the tumor was soft. I was so foggy, I didn't even get what that meant. Ashley nudged me and said, "Like Jell-O!"

Wow. That was one prayer answered.

I had been videoing the neurosurgeon at first, just like all the other times he met with me, but at some point I sat face to face with him, and Mattie had my phone. I don't even remember when I gave the phone to Mattie to video. It's probably a good thing I did give it to her, because the part where the neurosurgeon explained that Max was already *off the ventilator* and *pulling* at his oxygen mask with *both arms,* and I realized he was *not* completely *paralyzed,* I began to sob. Then, when the neurosurgeon told us that Max could *move both legs,* I'm pretty sure I hit my knees and screamed, "THANK YOU, JESUS!" and hugged the neurosurgeon.

I can't bring myself to watch that part of the video yet. I honestly can't bring myself to watch any of the videos yet. I think that is the most emotion I have ever felt in my whole life. Just typing this takes my breath. That moment is when the neurosurgeon explained that our best-case-scenario prayers had been answered.

He couldn't tell us a time frame on the tumor. He had no way to know if it had been there for months or years. He knew it wasn't weeks, though. He said if it had been there for weeks, Max's symptoms would've been a lot more severe. *But God* had him in the palm of His hand, just like He always has. The tumor was slow growing, and God had revealed it with perfect timing, as usual.

Bryan, Mattie, and I finally got to go to PICU to see Max. The first thing we noticed was that he had all of his hair! They parted his hair to make the incision so they didn't have to shave it off. We weren't expecting that! All of the kids in the PICU on the way in had big white bandages covering their heads. Not our baby—he looked just like he did when he left us at the OR doorway. He was awake and in so much pain. The first thing he asked was if they got it all. He leaned up off his pillow as much as he could and reached out to me. "Mama, did they get it all?" Those were his first words. Bless his heart.

I wasn't expecting him to be so alert, so aware of what was going on. I was so happy to hear him speak, I just cried. That first night was full of emotion. He was in so much pain—a pain that a mama, or daddy, or sister can't fix. They assured us that pain was a good thing, because it meant he was doing great. No pain meant there were complications in the brain. But, seeing your baby with a massive migraine (if you can even call it that) was tough. It was more than I could bear. It brought me to my knees (almost literally). I couldn't feel my arms or legs. The room felt like it was 150 degrees. I started seeing spots. I realized I was going to pass out. I was useless.

But God must've already planned for that, too. Bryan was there and his sister, Kristin, had come in at some point, too. I don't even remember her coming in. She helped Bryan take over. The nurses and doctors were in there talking, and I have no idea what they were saying, because I was about to pass out. I had barely eaten in four days, and I was emotionally exhausted. I felt like I was going to collapse.

How am I going to do this? How can I help him recover? How can I be strong when I'm so weak? How can I hold up my end of the deal with Max to be strong if I can't even stand? Lord, I need you. I need you so much. Help me get through this. He is in so much pain. I need help. So many thoughts ran through my mind as I sat in the corner trying to stay upright.

Bless Mattie's little heart. She stayed up with Max through the night. I was a mess. Bryan was exhausted. Max responded much better to Mattie than to us, so she sat with him for how many hours, I have no idea. I surrendered. I had to let God and Mattie take over in order to be worth anything to Max the next day. I guess Bryan felt the same way.

I woke up a few times in the night, and there my sweet baby

girl sat holding her baby brother's hand, trying to comfort him. I will forever have that image etched in my brain. It was just as heartwarming as it was heartbreaking. And again, I asked myself, *How can your worst day also be your best day?* Now I have an answer. *But God.*

Those next few days were rough. We weren't sure how long recovery would be, but Max was in so much pain. We had a different view of things than the nurses, though. They said he was doing so well the next morning that he needed to go back to the first floor. I felt confused. Max was unable to do anything on his own and was still crying in pain. He could barely sit up with support, and walking was super difficult.

The neurosurgeon vetoed him going back that soon, thank God. He said they wanted to send Max out of PICU because he was doing so well compared to most kids in the unit. He said they didn't understand how massive his surgery was, because he wasn't on a ventilator and was able to breathe on his own. Thank God for the neurosurgeon. A million times, THANK GOD!

The neurosurgeon wanted Max to get an MRI on Friday morning, less than twenty-four hours after surgery. They were going to do the MRI without sedation. I was a nervous wreck. Mattie was sleeping. Bryan had to go into work for a little bit. I was thinking I needed some strength from somewhere, but I didn't want anyone in the room with us besides Bryan and Mattie.

The night before in PICU, two nurses were in the room at the same time, and I told them both that they were taking care of a preacher. The short male night nurse seemed to understand what I meant when I said Max had just "told his preacher calling" over the summer. The tall male day nurse just kind of looked at me funny. I told them both that Max was going to be fine, because God was with him. Neither of them said anything to me, but they both smiled. I guess they get lots of crazy moms in the unit. Was I one of them? At that point, I felt like it most of the time.

We had the tall male day nurse on Friday. He could tell I was a hot mess. Max was in pain. We were having to put him on an MRI table awake. The last time he had been put on the MRI table awake, he got nauseated and they had to sedate him. I was told that he would not be sedated this time. The opening where they had gone in and performed surgery was on the lower back of his head and down into part of his neck. It was about four inches and had gone about two inches deep. His muscles were so sore, and to turn his head was excruciating. The opening for his head on the MRI table was going to make him lay his head directly on the part where he had his incision. He had around twenty-two staples holding it together.

Just the thought of that makes me cringe. Thank God, the tall day nurse finally figured out a medication combination that relieved Max's pain. He gave him a cocktail of morphine and acetaminophen that kicked in at just the right time.

We were about to go into the MRI room. The tall male day nurse must've been watching me looking at Max. I was actually praying with my eyes open. He asked me if I was okay. No one had actually asked me that that day. I teared up and said I wasn't okay. I told him I couldn't stand the thought of Max going through this, and he said something I didn't expect. He asked me if I remembered what I had told him the night before about Max being special and God having a plan for him. Once again, I was stopped in my tracks. I hadn't realized he was even really listening to me when I told him that. Yes, I remembered that, and yes, I needed that. I smiled and told him thanks.

The MRI went fine. Max was relaxed and rested the whole time. He didn't get dizzy or throw up.

From that point on, he just got better and better. On Saturday afternoon, they moved him out of PICU and back to room 114, just in time for Mattie's sixteenth birthday the next day. I had planned a small surprise party for Mattie for Sunday, but I had cancelled earlier that morning because at that time, Max was still not feeling well enough for company. We were all exhausted.

Max was starting to feel better, though, and had asked for pretzels—the first food he had requested since before surgery. Well, the wagons of food were in our car in the parking deck outside. So, Mattie and I went on a journey around the hospital to every floor with a vending machine. None of them had pretzels. So, to the car we went. She crawled around in the back of the car searching for a bag of pretzels. Thankfully, Emma, one of Max's favorite cousins, had visited before surgery and demanded that her mom go back into their house before they left and bag up some pretzel sticks to bring to Max. They had a goodie bag with all kinds of stuff in it that Emma knew Max liked, but Jodi, her mom, had forgotten to get pretzels. We laughed about that the day they brought them to Max. Now, Mattie and I laughed again as she crawled around in the car looking for that bag in the mounds of snacks. Finally, she found them.

We celebrated our find as we walked back to the hospital. Mattie seemed kind of sad, though. I asked her what was wrong, and of course she tried to make me believe she was fine. I knew she wasn't, and I knew it probably had something to do with her birthday being the next day. We were supposed to have had a big lake trip that weekend with all the Grant cousins and a few friends. The tumor cancelled that trip. Mattie and Max were both bummed about that.

So, I had to spill the beans on the surprise party we almost had in the hospital for her instead. She seemed like she was thinking about smiling at the thought of it, so the party was back on! I just had to see if Tracy and Amy could work some last-minute miracle and get the kids together. They did.

For Mattie's birthday, it was important to Bryan and me that we make it as special as a hospital birthday party could be. Not knowing how Max would feel, we wanted to try to stay close to the hospital and make sure we took turns with Max. Bryan and Mattie had spent the night the night before also. Max wanted us all together.

Bryan took Mattie to pet puppies at a pet store first thing when they woke up that morning. They didn't go to buy, just to pet, because puppies make everything better. I was going to take her to get a pedicure when they got back, but people had already started heading to the hospital, so it would have to wait.

While Bryan and Mattie were gone, I watched Max sleep. I was just praying he would wake up feeling like his old self for her birthday. Up until that point, he had a very flat affect. I thought (hoped) it was the morphine. There was a very good chance the surgery could've had an effect on his personality. I prayed that God would send me some kind of sign that the Max whom we loved so much would come back to us soon. He had such a big personality before surgery. Now, he was just kind of there. I was starting to get worried. He hadn't asked for Brendan or to play his favorite video game. He hadn't scared any of the nurses with the tiny sound machine my brother had given him his first night in the hospital. Before surgery, he had been using the sound machine to scare all of the nurses and to give everyone a big laugh. Where was that kid? *But God* wasn't done yet.

When he woke up, he seemed more alert. He was able to go to the bathroom a little better. He still needed help and wasn't very steady sitting up, *but God* is so good. I could see some progress. I was constantly reminded of the verse Casey, Bryan's friend who had passed from cancer, had loved, Isaiah 40:31: "But they that wait upon the Lord shall renew their strength; they shall mount up with wings as eagles; they shall run, and not be weary; and they shall walk, and not faint."

After we got him settled back in the bed, Max spoke in his normal voice for the first time. Sitting up, he looked at me and asked if he could play his favorite video game. One of his friends, AJ, and Mattie's friend Payton had set it up for him before surgery, but he hadn't played it yet. Of course, I turned it on and got him going. As he played, I told him we were throwing Mattie a birthday party. He asked if Brendan was coming. I almost cried. The two things I needed to hear from him, the two signs that I had asked God to give me, happened within minutes of him being awake. It was Sunday, and it was a good day.

We gave Mattie a small birthday party that day in the family room near 114 on the first floor. She didn't want to do anything that Max couldn't be a part of, so Tracy brought a few of Mattie's closest friends and a cookie cake. Amy brought Brendan and pizza. Not knowing how things would go, I only invited a few people who didn't have to be home at a certain time.

Max was able join us. It was the first time he had been in a wheelchair since surgery. He only stayed about ten minutes, but it was priceless. Brendan pushed him from his hospital room to the family room down the hall where the party was being held.

During the party, my phone rang. It was a number I didn't recognize, and I almost didn't answer. It was Tara Marcus, the doctor who had sent us to the ER for the CT scan. She had just heard about Max and was calling to check on him. I cried when I explained how her sending us to the ER saved him. She cried when she told me that she prays before every workday and asks God to guide her decisions. Then, I told her that I had prayed the Saturday before we saw her that God would help me get to the right person on Monday to get some answers. That person was her, and we will forever be grateful.

Chapter Ten

The Prayers

Pray without ceasing.

—1 Thessalonians 5:17

Max was able to come home the Tuesday after his surgery. From start to finish, he was in the hospital for nine days. He was no longer throwing up and dizzy. He was getting better every single day. According to the hospital therapy doctor, he needed occupational, speech, and physical therapy, but that could wait. We were headed home!

On the way home from the hospital for the first time, it was like we were bringing home a newborn baby again. We had to worry about his neck, just like we did when we brought him home for the first time. He could hold it up, but it was very weak. It seemed like every road we traveled on was under construction of some sort. I didn't think we would ever get out of Atlanta. He held his neck up with his hands the whole time. Mattie and I had bought him a stuffed dog in the hospital gift shop. He had used it to prop his head up in the hospital. He tried to use it in the car, but ended up using his hands. He had his eyes closed. He still had a pretty massive headache.

Things were very different at our house for several days. Max wasn't able to swallow his food that well. He would get choked on the medicine we gave him and throw up. Since the tumor was causing him to throw up for so long, any time he throws up now or even feels nauseated sets him into a panic that the tumor is back. We had to go to a swallow specialist to see if that was something he needed therapy for, or if his throat muscles were just slowly coming around, like his arm and leg muscles. Thankfully, it turned out that Max was still healing everywhere. He didn't need any special speech therapy for his throat. After a few days, his throat worked better. He had no appetite, but he could swallow better.

Max had some physical limitations. He could walk, but swerved to the left pretty badly. He could get up on his own, but it was very slowly, and his neck was so sore from the incision, he couldn't turn it much at all. He was in slow motion. He was also still having massive headaches. In order to move anywhere in the house, we had to help him up and guide him. He wore a belt around his waist that we were supposed to hold onto to keep him from falling. Yes, he was still a fall risk. He hated that belt, so he begged us not to make him wear it when we left the hospital. So, we held onto his arm or the back of his shirt.

It was slow going for several days. He didn't want us in the bathroom with him, so I was a nervous wreck thinking he was going to lose his balance and fall in the half bath he had been using in the kitchen. I could just see him toppling over and hitting his head. It gave me total anxiety.

Each day was better than the one before, but after a couple of days stressing over the bathroom situation, I had Bryan install handicapped handles on either side of the toilet in the hall bath. As he installed them, I prayed that God would heal Max and that he wouldn't need these handles for the rest of his life.

The next morning, Max's balance was so much better that I no longer had to hold him to go to the bathroom, and he didn't even need the handles Bryan had installed. Tell me God doesn't answer prayers. My baby is living proof.

Max "slept" in the living room. There wasn't a whole lot of sleeping going on. Turns out, the pain medication kept him restless. He couldn't sleep, which meant I couldn't sleep. He threw up a few times, too. We figured out it was just from the anesthesia, but for a while we had to carry the puke bucket everywhere we went. That was fun.

We moved the furniture out that wasn't needed. The rugs were all gone, too. We had to make the house easy for us to navigate him from the couch to the bathroom. I slept in the living room with him, too. It really was like having a newborn, making sure he was still breathing and getting up with him several times in the night. *But God* gave me strength. I wasn't even that tired. My strength sure didn't come from eating or sleeping, because I wasn't really doing much of either. Neither was Max.

We didn't allow visitors for several days. He was still gaining his strength and balance back. He wasn't sleeping. His head was killing him. We were keeping the house quiet and dark so if he ever was able to rest, he could. Those moments were rare.

Max was afraid this would be his life from now on. He had no appetite. He had no personality. He was physically worse off than before surgery. Although we had seen such great improvements, we still wondered if we would ever have our son back to normal again. I kept thinking back to something God had told me in the hospital. I had been so worried about Max's flat affect and lack of personality. *But God* told me I would get my son back one day, just like he was before surgery. At this point, though, it was really hard to continue to believe that was going to happen. He was getting better daily, so the prayers were working, but he was nowhere near recovered. I knew I was just being impatient and had faith and hope that God was going to keep His promise.

At some point, someone was supposed to call me to schedule a physical therapy (PT), occupational therapy (OT), and speech evaluation at the day therapy program down at Scottish Rite. This was kind of a sore subject. I had gotten into a disagreement with the therapy doctor before we left the hospital. She tried to tell me that Max was going to need day therapy for OT, PT, and speech, which meant going to therapy and school down at Scottish Rite from 9:00 a.m. to 3:00 p.m. every day. This opinion was based off of his OT and PT evaluation while he was in PICU less than forty-eight hours after brain surgery. She, herself, had not seen him do anything related to either of those areas, and speech had not evaluated him at all, so the special-educated-teacher/mama/advocate in me voiced my own opinion.

I knew we had so many people praying, and God had answered those prayers daily. From one day to the next, he was getting so much stronger. Max was already leaps and bounds ahead in all those areas from what they had prepared us for, so I felt like he wasn't going to need any of that therapy—not to that extent, anyway. So, she and I disagreed, and I basically left her with the "Well, we'll just see about that" mindset. She's the only person I had any trouble with while in the hospital. I was already sick and tired of doctors not listening to me from the year of "reflux." I guess I took all my frustration out on her.

I felt good about things, though. I knew God was going to help me prove her wrong. And He did.

One day, out of the blue, Max woke up and felt almost completely like his old self. He was going to the bathroom on his own, wanting to eat, bathe, and dress himself, and it seemed like everything was back to normal . . . except his personality and his left eye. He still had a very flat affect, and now his eye wasn't shutting all the way.

The eye thing was new. That was something that we didn't see happening in the hospital. He also couldn't see anything at a distance. It was blurry. It seemed to get worse every day. Other than the eye and vision, though, everything was almost back to normal. He wasn't super strong, but he could do almost everything physically that he could before. We were still praying about that and his personality.

Our appointment for the day-therapy evaluation ended up being exactly two weeks after surgery. They wanted us to come in a few days earlier, but I had already planned on taking Mattie to get her driver's license. She hadn't been able to get it for the first appointment we had made, because it was the day Max came home from the hospital. She was bummed, but a week later, she had her license and could drive!

Max was doing great by that point, except for his vision. His balance was normal, and he was walking and taking care of himself on his own. His personality was some better. So, as soon as we walked into the day-therapy office, the receptionist looked at us like we were lost. I told her Max's name, and she just stared at us strangely, but gave me the paperwork to complete.

Shortly after, someone took us to a room to weigh Max and take his blood pressure. The girl doing all that kept staring at him. I was trying to figure out why the first two people we saw were acting so weird. Maybe they thought he was as cute as I always have.

Then, the assistant to the therapy doctor with whom I had the disagreement in the hospital came in. After some small talk, she finally came out with why they were all looking at him. She didn't think he belonged there. *Finally!* I told her I couldn't agree more and that I had pretty much told the therapy doctor that in the hospital.

We went through with the evaluation anyway. We were there already, and I thought it was going to be good to confirm he was normal in all the ways I had noticed.

By lunch, someone came and talked to me. She told me that Max was not going to be a day-therapy patient. I told her that I knew that before we brought him. She was nice, and it was another opportunity for me to share God's grace and how all of North Georgia was praying for him.

The only therapy they recommended was PT, and it was only for balance on one foot with his eyes closed. Isn't that funny? You should try standing on one foot with your eyes closed. I can't do it, and I haven't had brain surgery. God is good! That one thing no one else can do was the only thing Max couldn't do, except close his left eye all the way and see clearly at a distance. We still had to get that situation figured out. I was not about to believe that we were done healing in that area.

I prayed day after day for God to grant me just one more prayer. A teenager's looks are important to him, and Max was starting to feel insecure. He had enough on his plate. He didn't need to worry about that eye. *But God* knew that already, too.

Even knowing all that God had done for us, the eye was worrying me a little. Some of the day-therapy patients had vision issues. You could see their brain-tumor removal scars on their heads, so I was so worried this would be the new normal for Max. The doctors we saw for therapy said that his vision weakness was due to where the tumor had been on his brain stem. They didn't give much hope for it to return to normal.

The eye doctor and massage therapist we saw did, though. They both gave us hope. We have been seeing the same eye doctor for years. I didn't know it when I made the appointment, but her husband had been diagnosed with cancer not too long before that. I found out recently that he passed away. She was so kind to us. She said she had seen people's vision improve after surgery. She said Max's vision weakness was caused by the anesthesia, and it would get better. The medical doctor he saw after that didn't seem to think so, but the eye doctor was right. It did improve. Max could see, but his eye was still not closing very well.

Max saw a massage therapist for several years to keep his asthma under control without medication. After we got home from the hospital, I took him in to see her for his asthma. She worked on Max's feet, back, neck, and lightly on his face. She wanted us to come back each week for the next few weeks for her to continue releasing the muscles in his neck and work on the nerves in his face. She felt like she could get that eye fixed. She kept telling me she could feel a difference, that he was healing. Her name was Hope, and she gave us hope.

All of the doctors we had seen after being home from surgery had not seemed hopeful the eye would get any better. They all had that look of pity, that look that me hoping for it to get better wasn't going to happen. I was not about to let that get to me. I had seen God work in the most awesome ways in the last few weeks, and we weren't going to give up just because a few doctors didn't see any hope for change. Doctors also hadn't thought Max had a tumor at one time.

Finally, we were rewarded for all our hoping and praying. After a few weeks, we realized the massage therapist was right. She had been saying all along it was going to heal. She had given us hope when no one else had, and Max's face and neck were healed. He could close his eye, and his neck was no longer stiff and sore. Hope was amazing—the person and the noun.

We kept all of our family and closest friends in the loop with updates of Max's daily or weekly progress. When a prayer was answered, we let them all know, so they knew God was hearing their prayers. We wanted everyone to know how they were in this with us and how we couldn't do it without them. I've never been a part of anything quite like it. We had so many kind people doing so many kind things for us. People sent cards, money, boxes of Jell-O with messages, bracelets with Bible verses inscribed on them. So many people were so kind.

There is no way to even begin to show how much we appreciate everything they did for us. But the prayers and strength—those were the most important things anyone did for us. We needed prayers and other people's strength to get through. I had people telling me they had been on their knees praying for Max each morning. Some people I don't even know (and don't know how they got my number) told me they were praying. It was like a prayer epidemic. It was so good.

Our baby had been in the fight of his life, *but God* is so good!

Chapter Eleven

The White Flag

Be still and know that I am God.

—Psalms 46:10

During a race, it is easy to lose track of how many laps you have done. Each lap, the riders go through the score tent to make sure their lap gets counted. When they have one lap left, the white flag is waved at the tent to let the racers know they need to give it everything they've got. The race is almost over.

There were so many times throughout this journey I wished someone was there to give me flags for signs; flags that would let me know how much more we had to go through before this race was over. But, just like in all other aspects of life outside of racing, God holds those flags, and we are supposed to trust Him to reveal them in His time.

With Max finally healing, it seemed like things were going to be okay. Then, we got the news that his radiation was going to have to be in Jacksonville, Florida. We had known radiation was definitely happening, because they had told us that from the beginning. Max's type of tumor had way better results of not coming back if radiation followed a full resection. So, finding out that radiation needed to be in Jacksonville, Florida, was a major letdown, since we had just gotten settled back in at home. Max had just started sleeping in his own bed. Things were finally getting back to normal.

Jacksonville? Why? We were just devastated.

That wasn't all. We had to take Max for a spinal tap. There was a chance that baby tumor cells were in his spinal fluid. If they were, then they had to radiate a larger area of his body than just where the original tumor had been.

Seriously? This isn't over yet? That's all we could think at the time.

We sent out another prayer request. We begged for people to pray that Max would not have baby tumor cells in his spinal fluid. It felt like this was never going to be over. We had so much for which to be thankful, and God had answered so many prayers already, it seemed selfish to ask for more prayers, but this was major. We needed prayers big time.

We had already been told the possible effects of radiation on the space where the tumor had been. They were pretty much the same possibilities as the complications Max could've had from surgery. There were also some serious possibilities with the spinal tap. It could cause a long list of scary things that I blocked out of my memory. I started to feel helpless. We had been on such a high from the surgery success and from Max improving so much. So many prayers were answered, yet it wasn't over. Would it ever end?

Long story short, the spinal tap went fine. Bryan's sister, Kristin, went with Max and me. She is a nurse practitioner and is very calming, so we thought she could keep us calm and help explain things. Max was sedated for the procedure, which took about fifteen minutes, and then we got to see him. He was so funny. He was saying all kinds of crazy things and had the nurses rolling in laughter.

We sent out another praise report to all our friends, family, and church family who had been praying for us. We were just amazed at God's grace.

Why does He keep answering prayers for our son? We knew how powerful God is, but how were we so blessed with such good results when others in our community hadn't been? A teenager who had been battling cancer for a few years in the county next to us had recently lost her battle. I couldn't even let my mind go to a place where that was our life.

Why is God so good to us? Why has He chosen US for this particular journey? How did we get so lucky? I was thankful, but didn't feel worthy.

Right before we left for Jacksonville, we received a call from the oncologist. The oncologist herself was on the other end of the phone. I was about to pass out. I was so worried that it was bad news. She had the results of the spinal tap and called us herself. At this point, doctors didn't call us; they made us come in or had someone else in their office call. As soon as she announced who she was, she just burst out with the news of the spinal tap. It was negative! No baby tumor cells. No cancer cells were in our baby's body! I'm not sure who was more excited about the news: the oncologist or me. She was beside herself! It was so overwhelmingly awesome, I don't even think I spoke. She had to tell me the news again to be sure I understood her. All I could think was, *Everyone who has been praying for us is going to be blown away by one more answered prayer.* They just kept coming!

We set out for Jacksonville, Florida, for almost eight weeks. Max and I were flying solo since Mattie had school and Bryan had work. My parents came with us, but it still felt like we were all alone. It wasn't anything they did wrong or didn't do; it was that half our hearts were still in Georgia with Bryan and Mattie. We are always together.

Why has God sent us so far from our family? When will this journey ever end?

I'm not going to lie. I was not in a good place. I had a smile on my face, and to the world I was being positive, but I was so very sad. I was leaving my baby girl and my husband, and it seemed like it was going to be forever. I didn't feel like God was with us anymore. I felt so alone.

Then, one day God said to me, "I'm not going to leave you now. I've been here this whole time. Just wait. You'll see there is a reason for your journey." It made me think back to a stranger who had given me scripture before we left for Jacksonville. He had been following Max's story through a mutual friend and felt led to give me scripture. He said, "God will never leave us." He wanted me to know that. God had sent that to him for me. If God cared enough to send scripture through a random stranger, then I could hang on just a little longer.

So, I tried to do just that. I waited. I wasn't happy, but I waited. I had almost lost the ability to feel my joy, but I waited.

Before we first left for Jacksonville, one of the ladies of the church Max was supposed to preach at in September contacted me online. Her name is Tina Brady. She said she was sending me a spiritual book she was reading that she thought I needed to read. It's about how God interrupts your life and how you may need to change your perspective. I thought to myself, *I do not like to read, but I'll be nice and take the book. I might read it, but I doubt it.* The book came to our house in the mail right before we left. I took it with me to Jax, even though I didn't see myself reading it. She said she had also given me access to the videos that go with the Bible study. *A video? That's way better than a book. I might be able to handle that.* I was definitely going to try to incorporate that Bible study into my routine in Jax. That was something that I knew I could do.

The first week we were in Jax was tough. Max and I both missed home. We missed Bryan and Mattie. We missed our beds, shower, and kitchen. He missed his dirt bike. I missed my couch. And, we missed things going on in our town and in our church. One thing we missed was Wednesday night services at church. We either have Bible study or choir practice. It hit me that I could do that Bible study Tina had sent me, and it might help me with ideas for our youth Bible study. *It might help my mood.*

I started the first video. It was about Jonah. As I listened to the lady talk, I realized it was something Max needed to hear, too, so I asked him to join me. He willingly did. I didn't really think much about the story of Jonah before then. *But God* had sent Jonah on a journey he didn't want to go on. Jonah ran from God, and that's how he ended up in the belly of the whale. He actually had a crew of a ship throw him overboard, because God had caused storms to develop out at sea to get Jonah's attention. He wanted Jonah to spread His word in Nineveh, but Jonah didn't want to go. *But God* gave him a second chance. He saved him from the whale.

Jonah's life had been interrupted by God, and mine had, too. At first I thought the Bible study was sent to me for Max, but the more I heard, I began thinking maybe it was for me.

We had five treatments out of thirty-three down when Max preached at Harmony at the end of September for their youth service. We weren't sure if he was going to be able to preach until the last minute. He could've easily used the radiation as an excuse not to, but the Friday before treatments started, we were listening to the Dawson County High School football game on the radio and he asked me what he should do about preaching at Harmony. I told him that was between him and God. He said he felt like he was supposed to preach that weekend if he felt like it, so I told him that if God allowed him to be healthy enough to travel, then that would be his answer.

I was so glad he was able to go. I had felt like that was what he was supposed to do all along, but when he first told me about his preacher calling, I told myself that I was not going to influence him in any way unless God sent me something. All God sent me was to leave it between Him and Max. So, I did.

Thankfully, I was able to talk to Tina when we first sat down that Sunday morning at Harmony, and I thanked her for including me in their Bible study. They were almost finished with the study, and I had barely started. I think I had watched only the first one at that time. She said that their first gathering for their first Bible study was August 13—the same day we found out about Max's tumor. She said when they heard the news, they stopped and prayed for us during their Bible study that night—another way God worked to create a detail to a story no man could ever create.

Max's message at Harmony was so sweet. He talked about how he was thankful that God had chosen him to be on this journey. He said he felt special. I felt honored to be his mom in that moment. He read from Philippians 4:9: "Those things, which ye have both learned, and received, and heard, and seen in me, do: and the God of peace shall be with you." He talked about how we had listened to our Jesus music when times were tough in the hospital. He talked about how blessed he had been to have had the tumor and be able to tell about it.

Before we got back to Georgia, Max had asked me if I thought it was okay if he just "talked" again. The first big crowd he had preached to was at our revival, and he "talked" about the story of his preacher calling. Now, he felt like God wanted him to "talk" about his tumor journey. He said, "Maybe I'm just going to be one of those preachers that talks." We've talked about what kind of preacher he was going to be several times since he told his calling. We had one preacher at our church who looked like a rooster when he got in the spirit. One said, "Whew!" with lots of expression. Our current preacher, Jason, is very active. He acts out a lot of scenes as he preaches. It really gives a good visual. So, we've wondered what Max will do when he gets in the spirit.

We went back to Jacksonville. We had twenty-eight treatments left, which seemed like an eternity.

On into our time there, God could see that I was in a bad place still. I could put on a fake smile and hide it from everyone else, *but God* knew. He started sending me signs. They came in a lot of ways. They came in the form of a cross from what looked like fence wood that had washed up on the beach after a storm (a storm that caused Max to have a migraine). Then, I saw another cross the next day on the beach. The strangest songs on the radio spoke to me and gave me hope—songs you wouldn't think would give hope. Random people would text me or call me at the most random times. That gave me hope. We would go home for the weekend and Bryan's dad, Randy, would bring a box of tacos. That would give me hope. I love tacos. He always came at just the right time, too. Other people would post things online that spoke to me. They didn't put them on there for me, but they spoke to me.

My favorite post was from one of my mom's oldest friend's daughter. She talked about how she had been in a funk, and God had "covered her with his feathers," like the scripture says. God had sent her signs that He was with her by allowing bird feathers to be in her path for twelve days, or something like that.

I hate birds. They freak me out, especially when they fly above my head within swooping distance. Swooping distance, to me, is when they are close enough that they could attack my neck. I feel like that is what they want to do. My granny had a crazy bird in her yard when we were little, and it would swoop down at us and try to peck us with its sharp little beak. And, I *hate* their claws. They make me shiver. So, I really do hate birds, but now I hate them a lot less. God sent me feathers for several days in a row while we were in Jax and I was in my funk. Every time I saw a feather on the ground, I would think back to that post describing the bird feathers and smile, knowing God was with me. I wasn't alone. This was going to end someday. He had us in His hands.

When we came home for the weekends between radiation treatments, we went to church. Jason's messages gave me hope. I don't remember what one was about exactly, but at some point in the message it hit me. I was sad, because I wanted my life to be back to normal. God told me that our life would never be the normal we knew before. He had changed our normal. He had interrupted our life to use us in a way to glorify Him. That's not something that normally happens in this large of a way for us. That message changed my perspective completely.

God had sent us to Jacksonville for a purpose. We were nearing the end of that journey, and the purpose would be revealed soon. I was so ready for it all to make sense, but I continued to wait. I knew I wouldn't have done the Jonah Bible study from home. That was definitely something I had to be set apart in order to have the time to do with an open mind, instead of an I-have-so-much-to-do-around-the-house-and-for-work mindset.

I will say, though, that God really showed out for me in the last year. I had two high schoolers seek me out for guidance, counseling, and I guess love. They had "stuff" going on in their personal lives that they just couldn't handle alone, and they basically needed to know from someone other than their parents that it was going to be okay. Why they chose me, I'll never know, but I let them know that they were loved unconditionally. That's what God wanted me to do.

I asked Him why he chose me over and over. *Why did you put these kids in my life at basically the same time? What can I do? I can't change their situations. I'm helpless in that way. Why me?*

Over and over in that still small voice, He would say, "Just love them." So, I did. I continued to love them and be there for them when they needed me. They also distracted me from the major issues that were obviously going on with Max that I wasn't supposed to see. I think had I not spent so much time praying and worrying about these two kids, I may have pushed for answers sooner, and we would not have found ourselves in the blessed situation that we are in now. Had we not been to see the right doctor at the right time in the right season, things could be very different for us. So, I am so thankful that God didn't allow me to abandon those two sweet kids. The good news is, they both got their situations figured out literally days before we found Max's tumor. Coincidence? Ha! No way. God was all over that timing.

Each week in Jacksonville, we had someone different coming either for the weekend or for the week. Every other weekend, we came home if Max felt like it. Mattie and some of her friends came for their fall break. Dawson County Schools had never had a full week for fall break until fall of 2018. Coincidence? Again, I think that was God. I was going to get a whole week with my baby girl. I was so excited, and so was Max.

Almost halfway through this Jacksonville journey, some of Max's friends came, too. His oldest friend, AJ, came. His mom was one of my best friends in high school. She and I have worked together in several jobs, too. We go way back, so naturally our boys were friends. They fight like brothers, too. He had another friend, Emma, come, too. Emma is actually his cousin. Her dad and I are third cousins, but our kids didn't really get to know each other until they went to the same middle school. Growing up, though, this cousin was my favorite human. We were born ten days apart and were the best of friends. So, it was very sweet that Emma and AJ were able to come.

Unfortunately, effects of Hurricane Michael joined us, even though it was on the Gulf Coast and we were on the Atlantic. It was the worst hurricane in the Mexico Beach area in one hundred years, predicted to knock towns off the map. Turns out, hurricane air pressure and Max's brain tumor don't mesh. We had no idea that hurricanes had any impact on his tumor (or the space healing where his tumor had been). But looking back, we had been impacted by two hurricanes in the two years prior to this one.

In 2016, we went to Jekyll Island right after a hurricane had passed through. Max threw up the whole time we were there. In 2017, Hurricane Irma impacted Georgia, and Max developed what we thought was a stomach bug. Now in 2018, Hurricane Michael was throwing pressure and storms our way, causing Max to have a massive migraine again. The second day that Mattie and the other fall breakers were there to visit us, Max woke up in the night feeling just like he did post–tumor removal in PICU. His neck and head hurt, and he was crying.

Great. Just great. Can't the poor kid get a break? I asked myself.

Now wide awake in the middle of the night, we tried to figure out what was going on. *Is his tumor back? Is the radiation causing this? Why is he suddenly back to square one? Why, God, why?*

And then, it hit me. Max had already made the connection that he threw up every time we took a long trip for Labor Day in the camper. He had determined (before this last headache) that it was the bouncing and laying down that caused pressure on his tumor, causing the nausea. The tumor was located on the "nausea" button on his brain stem, so that made total sense in hindsight. But now he was having pressure symptoms again. Why?

It finally came to me that the trips we had taken in September 2016 and 2017, and the Irmacane of 2017 had all included changes in barometric pressure due to hurricane season. The first time Max started vomiting was the morning after a treacherous thunderstorm. The Colorado trip had the opposite effect. It alleviated the pressure from his tumor. That's why he had no symptoms when he went on that trip.

Wow. Was I a genius? Maybe. Should I be in medical journals? Maybe. Time would tell. We wouldn't know until Hurricane Michael hit land and got out of our area to be sure. Of course, we discussed it with his proton doctor. He and Katie, Max's favorite nurse, were intrigued by my theory and said we would have to wait and see.

For the next two days, we did what you can do for a migraine. We gave him medicine and kept his head covered so the light wouldn't make it worse. Lo and behold, my theory was right. Once the hurricane was in North Georgia and completely out of the Florida area, Max felt good again. Thank God! Our fall-break plans were ruined, but his headache was gone, and we had at least connected a few dots that we wouldn't have without it happening.

Unfortunately, our favorite Mexico Beach house was badly damaged by Hurricane Michael. It was one of the lucky ones, though. It was still standing, but had lots of damage. So many houses and condos in that area are completely gone now, nothing there at all except flat ground. We had been vacationing there for twenty years and had so many memories there. It was our favorite area in Florida.

I began to wonder if that was why God had sent us to

Jacksonville. We were staying in an area on the beach called Ponte Vedra, Florida. We loved it. It was just enough like the Gulf beach areas we loved to feel like home. We were only a ten-minute drive from grocery and retail stores, yet we were in a secluded area where you might only see ten people on the beach all day. Was that the purpose in us coming to Jacksonville?

Many times, I sat by the ocean or on the porch and watched the waves come in and out. While I was there, Ashley gave me a book to read that made me think more about the waves than just how massive the ocean is. The book talked about how just like the waves are sure to come in with the tide, God's love is going to constantly be there. I needed to hear that. We were feeling so alone.

With that said, I love the beach and have often said that I could live there easily. Bryan and Mattie feel the same way. Was that why we were here? To see if we truly could live at the beach? I found out I could. I questioned God's method to the madness often, but I knew He had plans. That is the only thing that kept me going. Still does.

I continuously thought about what God's purpose could be for sending us to Jacksonville. I know everything happens for a reason. We were there because the proton-beam radiation was safer for Max, and that was great, but Atlanta would have a proton-beam radiation center in January. Why had God led doctors to find the tumor at a time that wouldn't allow us to use that facility? Why in the world did we have to come to Jacksonville and be away from all of our family and friends if the radiation could've been done at home a month or two later?

I knew in my head that if we had found the tumor later, Max could've had irreversible damage to his brain stem, and we would have had a completely different outcome. But, I also knew that

God could have held that tumor growth off until the timing was right for us to be able to do radiation in Georgia two hours from home. There was something bigger we were supposed to do or learn. There was someone we were supposed to be here for. What or who was it? We were nearing the last two weeks of our journey there, and I had no idea what God's plan was yet.

I had been able to be a part of some of God's plans in the last year. Totally unrelated to Max or anyone else in my family at all, but I had seen how God could work in other people's lives if you pray and wait. So, I was going to continue to pray and wait, although I was growing impatient and beginning to think I was just hoping for something that wasn't going to happen. I started to think that God was finished with our story, and we just had to get Max healed so he could preach. And, I was okay with that, although it seemed kind of like a non–Godlike ending to me. Usually, His ways seem like they have a bigger climax. Yes, the tumor was huge, but I just didn't get the feeling that was it or the end. I did feel like God was telling me there were no more tumors for our future, so maybe this was it. Maybe this was how the story would end.

Max and I continued the Jonah Bible study the whole time we were in Jacksonville. Of course, we could still relate with Jonah in that Max had run from his preacher calling and God had "interrupted" our life, but I was beginning to wonder if that was all we were supposed to get out of it. That was enough, but I just felt like it was going to have a bigger purpose when I started the journey and the study.

Then, week five in the Bible study happened. Week five made everything make sense. Week five in the Bible study was actually week six for us in Jax. Week five scared me a little.

In the week-five message, the lady told the study group that

God was telling Jonah, "Go and do what I asked you to do." She said it several times. The first time she said it, I thought, *Well, God hasn't really told me to do anything here yet. She's not talking to me. I'm waiting on signs of things I'm supposed to do while we are here, and other than telling people Max is a preacher, I haven't really felt led to do anything yet. This isn't about me. Maybe it is about Max.*

Max was sitting beside me on the couch and was emotionless, so I thought it wasn't him, either. He did the Bible studies with me, but later on would admit that they were meaningless to him. He said he didn't get anything out of them at all. I guess it's probably a good thing that my fourteen-year-old son didn't get much out of an adult women's Bible study. Ha! It was geared toward women and moms. He will never be either of the two.

We continued the study session, and the lady repeated what she had already said about going and doing what God asked you to do. Again, I tried to figure out what it was I hadn't done yet, if anything. I've learned to be pretty obedient in the last several years. God has rewarded my obedience with blessings so many times that I can't *not* be obedient most of the time.

Finally, God used that still small voice he always uses to give me a hint. "The book. Write the book." It was clearly God, because that was the furthest thing from my mind. I had been thinking in terms of projects for other people, participating in community service in Jax, joining a church for Wednesday nights, witnessing to people I met. None of that ever seemed right, though.

Oh. My. Goodness. He is seriously wanting me to finish the book I started about our journey!

I had a skeleton of a book started. I had worked on it our first two weeks being in Jax. I had an outline and a few chapters that seemed okay, but I had little to no desire to complete it. I'm telling y'all, I was not in a good place. I smiled a lot and found blessings in what I could, but I was truly saddened about having to miss out on so many things at home. I was down because I didn't understand why we were even here, and felt like maybe I had let the devil get to me so badly that God had given up on getting me to do what He wanted me to do. The worst part was seeing Max sad. I think I would've been much better off knowing he was happy here, but he wasn't happy.

So, to try to write a book that was supposed to represent all of God's love and grace for my family was tough. But, turns out it was exactly what I needed to get me out of the funk I had let the devil get me in.

With two and half weeks left in Jacksonville, I continued working on the book. I sat for hours typing, crying, and wiping mascara off my face. I would remember things I had left out and go back and revise sections. I typed more in two days than I had the first two weeks we were here when I started the book. I prayed that God would let me type the words that He wanted in there and nothing else. This was all to be His glory, not mine.

We had a week and a half left of radiation. There was a light at the end of the tunnel. Max and I were flying home for the last weekend in October. We had been in Jacksonville for six and a half weeks, and we were ready to be home again for a few days. The calendar worked out that we were able to drive home every other weekend up until this point. And, it was a long drive. Getting to fly home was going to be refreshing.

Tracey Phillips, the guy from our church that took Max and the Bethel Boys to his cabin in Colorado, had offered to fly us anytime we wanted. Personally, I do not like to fly, so I was fine with the long drive home, but Max *loved* flying with Tracey when they went to Colorado, and I *loved* anything that would put a smile on Max's face while we were in Jax. So, flying was what we were doing.

Thank God for putting us in the right church with the right people who love us enough to take time out of their busy lives for us. Tracey's daughter, Jessi, had brought a ridiculously large bag of food to us in the hospital. She worked at Georgia Tech in the drone department (she's really, really smart), and she and her mom thought we might be hungry. I think the exact words were, "I know how those Grants like to eat!" So funny.

Jessi and her mom, Lisa, had also brought Max a propeller and plaque from Jessi's drone department. It is hanging on his wall at home. Jessi is Jake's brother. Jake has loved Max since they went to Colorado. Every time I see or think of Jake's smile, it reminds me of when Max told his preacher calling, and that just makes me so proud and happy. That family has been such a blessing to us, like so many other families on this journey.

So, we flew home and it was actually pretty awesome. I felt like a celebrity. I thought to myself as we flew, *If the book sales go well, maybe we can get Max a plane someday.* That is laughable.

God quickly reminded me of the rest of the Bible study message in week five. The lady talked about how Jonah only had five words to say to the Ninevites when he got there. God had pulled him out of the belly of a whale to say five words. You would think a person coming to say five words would be laughed at, but God told Jonah not to worry; He'd take care of the rest. Jonah did his part, and God did His, too. Those five words Jonah had to tell the Ninevites would end up making a huge impact. Five words. I guess I shouldn't worry too much about this book not being very long. I was really kidding about buying a plane, but God must have some kind of plan for this story. In no way would I ever compare our story to the magnitude of the impact Jonah's has had on others, but if this book brings just one person closer to God, then it has all been worth it.

While home for the weekend, we went to church. We went for the fall carnival Saturday night and for the church service Sunday. It was such a blessing to be able to do that. I am constantly reminding myself how each little normal thing we do is a blessing.

I noticed they are building a really long wheelchair ramp in the new construction at the church. I couldn't help but think about how glad I am that we would not have to use that ramp when it is finished. My baby will get to use the steps like he always has. It is a blessing that we are not pushing Max in a wheelchair with a ventilator and a feeding tube. It is a blessing that we aren't having to buy a car that has a wheelchair ramp. It is a blessing that our insurance covered most of our hospital bills and we don't have to sell our home to be able to pay the bills. It is a blessing that the place we stayed in at the beach is right on the beach and we were able to afford that. That beach view got me through many more tough times than I realized it would.

We decided to stay at the beach instead of Downtown Jacksonville because we wanted this to seem more like a vacation, where we have to go do a little thing each day, instead of a radiation trip, where we might get to see the beach once in a while. And, our plan worked. Although we have let the devil work on us a little more than I would like to admit, we've really enjoyed the beach. We are simply blessed.

At church that Sunday, we sat across the room from Max, where Tracey and Lisa and their family usually sit. Mattie was asked if she would sing two verses of a song with two girls at our church. The rest of the youth choir was going to sing the chorus. To my surprise, my Mattie agreed. She usually doesn't like to be put on the spot like that. This journey changed her, too. She read over her verses while we sang the class songs and they took up the offering. She didn't even seem nervous.

I glanced at the song, but didn't think much of it. I've heard them sing so many songs in the past. They all start to run together in my head, so I was just waiting to hear it all put together with the kids and the guitar. I honestly couldn't place the tune by looking at it on the paper.

The youth choir director spoke to the church before the kids sang. She talked about how blessed our church was with so many youths. She talked about how blessed she was to see all the youths the day before at the fall carnival. And, she talked about what a blessing it was to see Max being able to enjoy himself. That was an understatement. It was truly a blessing to have him be able to enjoy it independently, just like he had before the surgery and radiation started.

It wasn't too long into the first couple of verses that I realized what I was listening to. They were singing "I Have Been Blessed." One of the other girls whom Mattie was singing with sang the first verse. Then, all of the kids joined in for the chorus.

By the end of the first verse, I was already tearing up. I had missed being at home, but I was still blessed. The verse about the pen of the writer got to me a little, since I had really been working overtime on the book. I thought about how blessed I was to be able to see Max walk, talk, breathe, eat, and use his arms. I was just blessed.

Then, my Mattie started in on the second verse for her solo, and I completely lost it. I hadn't even read her part before. When I glanced over the first line or two and realized I couldn't place the song, I had stopped reading. Her voice sounded angelic, and the words were so perfectly appropriate for our family. Her verse was about a voice that can talk, hands that can touch, legs that can walk, ears that can hear, and eyes that can see. We were so blessed that Max could do all of those things!

God loves us so much that He healed our baby and gave us a

purpose—a big purpose. I knew our purpose was to be a light to others, to write this book to share what God had done in our lives. I knew I had to work like crazy to finish it. God had separated me from my home and sent us to Jax so I could focus on this book. I wouldn't have even started it if I had been at home. He works in such mysterious ways.

Jason's message that followed the youth choir was very appropriate, too. The basic message that God intended for me to hear was "The journey is too great for thee to go alone." Thankfully, I knew I wasn't alone. I hadn't been alone. God had been with us, patiently waiting for Max and me to get our hearts right in order to be a light to others when we get home. We could do that. God had gotten us through the hardest parts. Our preacher's son even had bracelets made with Max's first message had had preached on them. They said, "He'll bring you through it - Max 316." People still wear them today. It just warms my heart to see them on their arms when we go out in public.

We got back to Jacksonville and felt like we could do this thing finally. Max had nine treatments left, and we could see the light at the end of the tunnel. It's funny that we talk about a light at the end of the tunnel a lot. The MRI machine has a tunnel. Looks like we will get to see that tunnel a lot in the next few years for rechecks, but there are worse things.

Halloween marked Max's twenty-eighth treatment. I love Halloween. Always have. I love the spooky stuff and dressing up. My kids, not so much. I wanted Max to dress like his proton-treatment doctor. He was about the same size as Max and wore a fitted button-up shirt, bowtie, and skinny khakis every single time we saw him. He was always fashionable. I thought it would be so funny, but no. Max wouldn't dress up. So, I decided we would go as tourists. That's basically what we were, anyway.

When we came in the door to the proton treatment center, I saw several kids dressed up. Some staff members were walking around dressed up as trophies in gold spray paint. They had put spider webs all over the receptionist desk. There were several older people in the lobby area who weren't dressed up, either. I noticed that the double doors to radiation or the doctor's offices had some kind of plastic covering. At first glance, it looked like some kind of plastic tablecloth. I didn't really pay attention to what it was, though.

Max signed in on the computer, and we went to our usual spot on a couch between the bathroom and elevator. We sat in that spot for two reasons. One is because there is an outlet, in case his computer or phone died. He works on his schoolwork while we wait to be seen. Sometimes we've waited for two or three hours to be seen, so he can get lots done in that lobby. The other reason we sat over there is because it is quiet and near the bathrooms. He can think, and I can, too. All the rest of the seating is across the room past the receptionist desk. There are usually lots of people over there, and honestly Max and I aren't small-talk kind of people.

As we sat there watching people come in all dressed up, I began looking around to see if they had decorated anything except those double doors and the receptionist desk. They hadn't. I looked back at the double doors to see what was on there. I couldn't believe what I was seeing! It was like another sign from God. I had waited this whole time to get a sign that we were in the right place with the radiation treatment. Finally, there was something that might give me an idea that this was part of the plan in some way, and there would be more to come.

The double doors were decorated like Noah's ark. For real. And, the staff were all dressed up like animals, two of each. Wow!

God was in this place the whole time. They had probably been planning that for a while. This inspired me to hurry up and finish my book. God was all kinds of in this thing.

On the day-thirty treatment, we met with our doctor and Max's favorite nurse, Katie. We went through the usual "How are things going?" conversations. Everything was good except a little hair loss around the incision spot, where they were directing the radiation. That was exactly why Bryan and I chose Jacksonville for treatments. We wanted Max to have as easy of a time as possible. So far, so good.

Katie, the nurse, was Max's best buddy from the start. They talked shark teeth on our first visit, and from then on a shark-tooth friendship developed. She loved looking for shark teeth at the beach, and so did he. One day, she gave him some tips. She even brought him one of her biggest, and challenged him to find one that size or bigger. It was a long tooth, so it was quite the challenge.

I shouldn't get surprised anymore, but that afternoon when we went down to the beach, he found one. We hadn't been there two minutes, and Max had found a great white shark tooth. It was wider and longer than all the others, exactly the same length as the one Katie had given him. He was so happy. He couldn't wait to take it back and show Katie. She was really impressed the next time we saw her at radiation.

So, on our treatment-thirty doctor's visit, Katie had a new challenge for Max. On the last day of his treatments, treatment thirty-three, he would get to ring the big windchimes in the lobby of the Proton Therapy Institute. She challenged him to ring the chimes louder and longer than anyone ever had. She challenged him to ring it so loud and long, people could hear it all over the building.

At this point, Max had never heard or seen the chimes

before. As she stood there, someone rang the chimes, and he got to hear it for the first time. This person only rang it once, and it didn't chime for long at all—maybe five seconds total. Katie challenged him to do better than that. Max had a twinkle in his eye as he thought about whether or not he was going to honor her request.

Bryan and Mattie had been down the weekend before the last treatment. They took all the things we didn't need for the last few days back home with them. We wanted to load as much as we could so our final load to go home would be as easy as possible for Max and me. Several people had given me books to read, but I knew I wasn't going to have time to read them those last few days, so I sent them back with Bryan. In that stack was the daily devotion book that had been so inspirational to us on surgery day. The scripture for surgery day was so perfectly placed in the book that it had to have been a God thing. I just couldn't send it in that bag to go home before me. I needed to hang onto it, even if I didn't have time to read it.

As we left for treatment number thirty-two, something told me to grab it. I needed to write a few thank-you cards, so I thought I could at least bear down on it. I had opened it a few times while we had been in Jax, but it didn't inspire me quite like the first time on surgery day. The few days I had read it were all about how to cope with death. Given our situation, that was somewhere I wasn't allowing my mind to go, so I had decided to stop reading it for a while. Bearing down on it for thank-you cards seemed like the best use of it at the time.

Radiation was on a hundred-minute delay for treatment thirty-two. Not surprising. This usually happened at least once a week. So, I had extra time on my hands. I thought I might work on the book while I waited. I had fine-tuned most of it, but God wouldn't tell me it was finished yet. So, I thought I could use this time to double check things.

As I dug in my bag for the computer, I ran across the devotion book. Out of curiosity, I checked to see what day thirty-three of treatment, the final day, had to say. Once again, God wowed me. It was titled "What is Joy?" I almost had a breakdown right in the lobby waiting area, but I managed to hold it together.

Joy had been a recurring theme for this journey. I began reading the November 7 devotion, the final radiation-day devotion. The scripture was part of Nehemiah 8:10: "For the joy of the LORD is your strength." That couldn't have been more perfect scripture for this journey, this race. God had shown us such grace that we couldn't help but be strong and try to find joy from deep within to allow us to be joyful. It was difficult at times, but I realized (maybe later than I would like to admit) that the devil was trying to steal our joy.

The devotion went on to talk about how some people think that just because you are a Christian, you should always be happy without any problems in your life. It went on to talk about all the times mentioned in the Bible where Jesus was sad about certain things. Things were not always perfect for Him. It basically combined the message that the young preacher at church camp had preached about joy and the message that our preacher, Jason, had preached one Sunday we were home from Jax. Nothing can ever rob us of the joy God gives us. Nothing. True joy radiates from within. Even Jesus suffered while on this Earth. God could've saved him from it, and we are supposed to have moments when everything doesn't go right. Those are the moments when we rely on God the most. Those are the moments where someday our story will help others.

Wow. Perfect. I sat there in awe of this devotion book. It was

Billy Graham's words of wisdom. He had passed away earlier in the year. After Max's preacher calling, someone had heard him preach for the first time and told me, "He could be the next Billy Graham." I don't know how that will go, *but God* does.

As I sat there trying to gather my thoughts about how to incorporate this into my book, I flipped the devotion book over, hoping the back was blank and I could stare blankly into it. There was writing on the back, too. It was Romans 15:13: "Now the God of hope fill you with all joy and peace in believing, that ye may abound in hope, through the power of the Holy Ghost."

No scripture was more perfect for how this journey, this race, this whole thing had been. We had been given peace since the beginning that God had this—a peace we couldn't explain; a peace that could only have come from one source: God.

Finally, day thirty-three of radiation arrived. It was a day that at one time didn't seem like it would get here soon enough, but now, I almost wanted it to slow down. As much as we had looked forward to the end, it was going to be a sad day. We had grown to love so many of the staff members at University of Florida Proton Therapy Institute. So many of them had been so kind to Max and me. So many of them had become like family.

It was finally Max's turn to ring those chimes in the lobby. The chimes are as tall as the average adult male and are suspended by thick metal wires on each side. They hover over a baby grand piano in the center of the room. No one ever played that piano while we were there, but I did see someone come tune it one day. At that moment, I really wished I had stuck with piano lessons as a teenager. Playing the piano would've been a great way to pass the time! It made a really nice centerpiece for the room, though.

I had seen so many others ring those chimes. Each time someone rang them, I cried. It signified the end of the radiation journey for them. When they rang them, the whole room would erupt in applause. Some people stood; some people sat quietly watching; some people stopped in their tracks to see the newest member of the I Survived Radiation Club. Max was going to be one of the next members of that club, and I found myself fighting back tears from the time I walked in the door that day until the time he rang the chimes. I felt very much the same as I had felt the first time I had heard him preach. It was like I was in a total world of my own.

During my time in the radiation waiting room, I had seen all kinds of approaches to ringing those chimes. The little kids barely rang them; the teenagers usually barely rang them; the younger adults would ring them a little longer than the teens; the really old people would do one of two things: barely a ding or a big ring. My favorite person that rang the bell was a gentleman in his sixties. He had a big group of people with him. He also had several staff members come watch him ring the chimes. He rang the heck out of them, and then he told everyone in the room how God was good and he could get you through anything. Anything! He kept saying that over and over. He pointed his finger across the crowd that had gathered and let everyone know where his source of strength came from. All of the ladies who came to see him ring the chimes were crying. I imagine that some were his daughters. One looked like maybe his wife. Several of the staff cried with them. It was such a sweet moment, I had to look away. I couldn't focus solely on it because I was afraid I would start crying and not be able to stop. Everyone there always seemed so well put together. You never saw anyone crying or sad. I guess they were like me: happy to be at this stage of the journey; happy to have some hope.

But, hope was overwhelming to me. That hope is what made me cry. I was so overwhelmed by the goodness of God, I just cried sometimes. To see someone else overwhelmed, like the older gentleman was that day, made me struggle to keep it together. He knew what God had done for him, and he wasn't afraid to tell everyone about it. It was definitely a very sweet and surreal moment.

Max's final radiation day went off without a hitch. The machines didn't break down. They ran on time. He got in and out. Then, we saw his doctor for the last time. Finally, it was time to ring the chimes. Thankfully, my parents, my sister, Bryan's mom, Bryan's sister and her girls, and almost all of Max's favorite therapy staff members were able to watch him ring the chimes. He did so good when he rang them. I think it helped that a girl about his age rang them right before him, and he tried not to get shown up by her. He rang them for a good, solid fifteen seconds. That doesn't seem like much, but in radiation chime time, it's a good one!

I've never been there when people cheer out loud. Usually, people just clap. This time, there was lots of cheering. Max did a little clap after he was finished and looked down at the ground as if praising God silently. Of course, I cried. He then went around hugging all of the people who had come to see him ring the chimes.

Bryan and Mattie weren't able to be there. He had work, and she couldn't miss any more school. She had some tough classes that semester. So, my sister and Bryan's sister video-called them. I held my tears pretty well until I saw Mattie's face after the chimes were rung. She was only able to hear it, not see it. She had a poor connection. She cried, and it killed me that I couldn't be there to hug her. This whole time, that was the worst part: not being able to be there to comfort her. Bryan was pretty strong, and Mattie had been putting on a good face, but I knew deep down that all of this was killing her. Finally, on chimes day, it was confirmed.

Thankfully, it would be the last time I wouldn't be able to comfort her in person. We were Georgia bound after we said all of our goodbyes.

Saying goodbye to our proton family was a lot harder than I thought it would be. They had been there for us when our family couldn't be. We had written thank-you cards for each of the ones who meant so much to us. There were five people whom Max wanted to give the bracelets that the church had made, the ones that said, "He'll bring you through it - Max 316." I wrote in the card that Max had preached about whatever difficult times God sends your way, He will bring you through those times. I wrote that God sent them to us to help us through this difficult time, and we thanked them for that.

Katie's card was different, though. Katie had a special bond with Max with their love of shark teeth. We had a special request of her. My friend Ashley had given us pennies to throw into the ocean after each treatment, one for Max and one for me. We had done this every day for thirty-two treatments, but this last treatment was going to be different. We were headed home to Georgia, not back to the beach where we had been staying. We weren't going to be able to throw our pennies, and we didn't want to throw them early. So, we put them in the envelope with Katie's bracelet, and her card had something added to it. We asked her to throw the pennies the next time she went shark-tooth hunting. I cried the whole time I wrote that card. It meant so much to me that she took the time to make Max feel special. It was so important to him to feel loved while at radiation. She did that. I will forever be grateful to her and all the other staff who loved us when our families weren't around to do that.

After Max rang the bell, we took lots of pictures and drove home to Georgia in record time. We only stopped once for food and gas, then we put the pedal to the metal and got home as fast as we could. It rained from below Atlanta all the way home, but we didn't even mind. We were headed home!

We had no idea that Bryan's aunts had painted "Welcome Home!" signs. They put one at the building supply where Bryan's family works. That was the first one we saw. We stopped to give Bryan a hug for a few minutes, then headed home. On our road, we saw the second sign at Bryan's sister's house (our old house), then his mom's house, then finally at our house. Bryan's aunts had hand-painted signs to go at the end of all those driveways.

When we got home, Mattie was there. She was so excited to see us, and we were so excited to see her. Bryan's cousin Cody had been at the building supply when we stopped by, and he followed us home to help us unload the car. I don't know how people who don't have family do things like this. We are so blessed.

It wasn't long until Bryan's Aunt Judy, one of the sign makers, showed up. She had eleven balloons and more signs to put up. When we went outside to meet her, we saw the most beautiful rainbow I have ever seen in my life. It circled over our whole house!

In the distance, we could see the brightest sunset I've ever seen at our house, too. The sky looked golden, it was so bright. It was like a gift from God letting us know everything was going to be okay from that point on.

Just like the rainbow He had sent Noah.

Chapter Twelve

The Checkered Flag

Wherefore seeing we also are compassed about with so great a cloud of witnesses, let us lay aside every weight, and the sin which doth so easily beset us, and let us run with patience the race that is set before us, [2]Looking unto Jesus the author and finisher of our faith; who for the joy that was set before him endured the cross, despising the shame, and is set down at the right hand of the throne of God.

—Hebrews 12:1–2

Just like in a race when you come across the finish line for the last time, the checkered flag was finally thrown. This race we were in was over. We were home, and slowly realizing that we didn't have to go back to Jacksonville.

Max was 100 percent himself. In fact, he was a new-and-improved version of his old self. He was physically, cognitively, and socially back. That was overwhelming to even type! There were so many times we weren't sure this day would ever come. There were so many times we didn't think our life would ever get back to normal. *But God* knew.

Y'all, God is so good. Max was such a trooper. He was an inspiration throughout the whole journey and so strong the whole time. He fought to live. He gave it everything he had. Just like in his races where he had charged to win the whole race, he charged to win this tumor battle.

Sure, he had moments of being really tired of our new normal, but within minutes he realized how much he had to be thankful for, and was positive again. That only happened a few times. He kept me strong right up until the finish line. We leaned on each other, and Bryan and Mattie were a source of strength when neither Max nor I could hold each other up. Bryan would remind us of all the reasons we needed to be strong. Mattie kept the house going and was there any time we needed her. She put her teenager needs/wants on hold for Max.

Other people sent random texts or messages of strength, too. It took a whole team, just like a pit crew in a race, to get us through this. We knew all the things they would tell us, *but God* sent messages through people we loved to confirm it. And, it was always at just the right time.

Let me tell you some things I've learned about His timing through this journey. I've had a lot of time to sit and think while not writing this book, because I stuck my head in the sand feeling sorry for myself. Often while I was thinking, God would send little things to keep me going and make me see the good in situations. If I stuck my head back in the sand, he would send me another reason I should be thankful for His timing. I'll try my best to make these make sense to you.

The timing in finding the tumor amazes me. Had we found the tumor any sooner, so many things would've been more difficult for us. If we had found the tumor last May, when the vomiting started, we would've been staying in Jacksonville for radiation during the busiest season for the beach. Most likely, we wouldn't have been able to find a place to rent that was near the beach, and we would not have been able to wake up and see the ocean every day. That view did so much for our souls while we were there.

Also, if we had found the tumor last May, Mattie would only

have been fourteen. She wouldn't have been able to drive herself to do things with her friends, like she can now, and her life would've been way less fun. That would've made everything worse for everyone. Max already felt guilty for us having to come to Jacksonville, even though he had zero control over it. Not only was she able to drive, but she got her license just in time to drive herself home from school before we left for Jacksonville. Her friend Payton took her home for a few days while we were in the hospital and the week after we got home, but she got her license that following week. She already had a car, because we had felt led to get her one right after she turned fifteen so she could get used to driving it. So, we weren't having to worry about car shopping during a hospitalization, either.

My parents were both retired and could come to Jacksonville with us, so that was a blessing. Had we found the tumor too many years earlier, they wouldn't have been able to come, and Max and I would've been alone in Jax with him at a much younger age. Bryan's mom, Sue, kept our kids when they were younger. Both my parents worked still, so they didn't get to spend as much time with them. I always felt bad about that. Sue was amazing and still is. She helped keep things going at home while I was in Jax. But, it was so nice that my parents were able to be with us during our time in Jacksonville.

If we had found the tumor over a year ago, when the symptoms first started, we may have been here in Jacksonville when Hurricane Irma came through and flooded the city. That may have impacted Max's radiation time and extended our time in Jacksonville. I am very thankful for that not happening.

We also found the tumor just in time for him to be home from the hospital and ready to go camping for Labor Day. That trip had been planned for months. The kids were looking so forward to it, because all the Grant cousins and Crane family would be there. The Cranes are family friends whom we consider family. Max was able to go on that trip and ride the jet ski. That was all he had talked about for weeks. He had regained his strength in mobility just in time to enjoy that trip. God is so good!

The radiation was during the time of year that there are no holidays. The only holiday that we weren't home for was Halloween. I'm not even sure we can consider it a holiday, but it's Max's least favorite, so it was a good one to miss. We were also perfectly timed to be back for Thanksgiving. We came home two weeks and one day before that special holiday. If that's not something to be thankful for, then I don't know what is. We ended up taking a trip to Mexico Beach in our camper with twelve Grant cousins to see the destruction. Max had been wanting to go so badly. Thankfully, we were able to, and it was a trip none of us will ever forget.

Most of all, had we found the tumor sooner, Max may not have told his preacher calling when he did, and we would've missed out on so many blessings that his calling has already brought. With a different doctor and a different team, we could've possibly had a very different outcome from surgery, and that could have affected his preacher calling or changed his ability to speak, for that matter. For that, I will forever be grateful.

Max will also be able to get his learner's license on time. Had the tumor been found later, he could've still been recovering, and that would've delayed him getting his learner's permit, which would've devastated him. He's been trying to get us to let him drive since Mattie turned fifteen and got her learner's license. God didn't take that from him, and we are so thankful for that, too!

So, here we are at the finish line of this particular race, wondering what is next. Is this it? Are we done with the tumor business? Are we on to greater things? We have no idea, *but God* does. And, he has been and will be with us the whole journey through.

We had been home a little over a week when I thought the book was finished. I kept waiting on a sign or a whisper from God letting me know the book was complete. I knew He would tell me it was finished when it was finished. I kept thinking of things that I might need to add, but none of them seemed like something I should drop everything and add to the book. So, I just waited. Finally, the sign I had been waiting for came.

I got a message from my friend Ashley. She sent me a story she had just read and said, "God is in everything if we just let him be." The story was about pennies. She was the one who had sent the pennies with us to throw in the ocean, so if the story was meaningful to her, I knew it would be meaningful to me. It was a tradition for her family to throw a penny for good luck into the ocean when they left their beach house each summer in Mexico Beach. She had given Max and me the pennies for our journey for good luck. Then, this story changed both of our outlooks on the pennies.

The story is about a very wealthy man who picked up pennies he found wherever he saw them on the ground. A woman bothered by him picking up pennies when he was so wealthy asked him why he would take the time to pick them up. She thought maybe he had a coin collection. His response was eye-opening for the lady in the story and brought tears to my eyes. I knew this was what God had had me wait for. I knew this *had* to go in the book.

The man pointed out four words on the penny: In God We Trust.

From day one in the ER when we first learned of Max's tumor, God had been with us. We knew that. We trusted that this was part of His plan for Max all along. We knew the whole time in

Jacksonville that God was with us, and we had religiously thrown our pennies in the ocean each day. The whole time the pennies had sent a message that Max and I never really even knew we were sending. In God we DID trust! Completely. Even on our bad days. Even on the days where we missed home so badly, it physically hurt. Even when we longed for this journey to end, we trusted God completely. We knew He was all in this thing. And, even on all those days of not feeling very joyous, we threw those pennies that carried such a literal and spiritual message. We trusted wholeheartedly. Even when we didn't like the path He had us on, we trusted Him.

The man went on to tell the woman that each time he picked up a penny, it was a symbol of the trust he had in God. Max and I had no idea we were even showing that trust by throwing those pennies, but something compelled us to do it each day. That was God compelling us all along. God knew the significance of that gesture even before we did.

The woman who wrote the story ended it with how she had found an endless amount of pennies lately. That was funny to me. There had been a penny laying outside my classroom since I had gotten back to work. No one had picked it up, including me. I will never leave another penny, even if it's on tails. Pennies will forever have a new meaning to me. I will forever remember the story of the man who had all the riches in the world, but still knew who all his blessings came from: God.

EPILOGUE

But none of these things move me, neither count I my life dear unto myself, so that I might finish my course with joy, and the ministry, which I have received of the Lord Jesus, to testify the gospel of the grace of God.

—Acts 20:24

There was still the question I had been asking from the beginning of our journey: *How in the world am I going to get this book published? Who is going to help me edit and make it make sense?*

I knew God was going to send me someone. He had told me to just wait and be patient. Every moment when I should've been working on the book during our two weeks in Jacksonville was an opportunity for God to speak to me in that still small voice, saying, "Work on the book." I heard it every single time I wasn't working on the book, but could've been. So, I finally listened. I typed constantly and prayed that God would give me what He wanted it to say. And, He did.

Finally, one day that last full week we were in Jacksonville, the helper I needed came to my mind. As I drove to radiation, I reflected over the weekend and how church had gone. I thought about how blessed I was that Max was able to work on his schoolwork on our way to radiation, and I wasn't having to help him that much. The pictures we were painted of possibilities of effects of radiation were not pretty, so I was thankful he was able to work alone.

Max was working, and I was listening to the radio and thinking about our journey when I saw that the song on the radio was by the band Journey. That was a coincidence. I turned it up a little so I could hear it better. It was "Don't Stop Believing."

Wow. Is that a coincidence? I teared up a little. I do that a lot now that I'm a pediatric-brain-tumor-survivor's mom.

I went back to thinking about Jason's message about the race and journey from a few weeks ago, and that led me to think about how blessed we are to have him as our preacher. His messages are so clear and relevant each time. I then thought about how his son, Luke, had helped design the bracelets that people were wearing to remember to pray for Max. My thoughts then shifted to how Beth, his wife, was also a coworker of mine now that I was at the high school, and that God really knew what he was doing moving me to the high school. The change from fourteen years at the elementary school as a special-education teacher to my new job of three years as a high school early-childhood-education teacher was just the breath of fresh air that I needed, and I knew that I would've been way more stressed in Jacksonville if I were still at the elementary school.

That change had been such a hard decision for me. My last few years at the elementary school had been so very stressful. Anyone teaching in elementary school—or even worse, elementary special education—can vouch for how much work goes into making sure all those babies are learning. It's rewarding, but exhausting. My last year at the elementary school will forever be etched in my mind as the worst year of my professional life. I had some difficult situations to work through as a teacher. I love my students like they are my own, and I always want to treat them like they are my own children. Sometimes, factors that are out of my control get in the way of that. So, I had prayed every morning on my way to work for God to intervene and help me find a way to find joy; either move me or change me. Mattie and Max were both in middle school at the time, so Bryan was taking them to school each morning. That was the start of my favorite time of the day with God. I was so used to having at least one kid in the car with me in the mornings, so when I didn't, I began talking to God. Once my job started getting so stressful, I began asking God to change the situation or change my heart.

We are in school 190 days as teachers. I talked to God at least 150 of those 190 days. The summer after is when I got the call that I had been waiting for: the early-childhood-education classes at the high school needed a teacher, and they thought I would be good for the job. I instantly started crying on the phone. An overwhelming feeling came over me, because I had been praying for God to rescue me or change me for ten months straight. The wait was over; I was being rescued!

But God knew there was going to be so much more to the story. I was going to *need* the people at Dawson County High School way more than I realized. I left an elementary school that felt like family worried that I wouldn't have those relationships form at the high school. God knew I would not need to worry. They took me in like family immediately. Beth was one of those people. Not only were we church family, we were work family now, too.

It's just overwhelming how God works in our lives.

That led me to thinking about Beth changing positions in the high school this year and being less stressed. She had been the yearbook advisor, a stressful position. Well, lo and behold, that led me to thinking that Beth knew about publishing and editing, and so could edit my book.

What in the world? God had gone and wowed me again!

I knew I was on the right track, because when I'm on the right track and an idea like that pops into my head, I immediately cry overwhelmed tears. I'm not sure what else to call it, but when God works in your life when you least expect it, you get overwhelmed in a good way, and when I get overwhelmed in a good (or bad) way, I cry. So, I cried the whole way to radiation.

Once we got to radiation, I sent Beth a text and told her I needed her editing skills. I knew she was competitive and would do a good job, but I also knew she had been one of our biggest cheerleaders throughout this journey and would know if something I wrote didn't make sense. So, I shared my very raw and unfinished manuscript with her.

Later that night, she sent me a text saying she had read the whole thing and cried . . . a lot. In my head I thought, *Well, emotion from a book is a good thing!* So, maybe I had done *some* justice for God.

She and I texted back and forth about me wanting her to be yearbook advisor/editor Beth when she read it instead of church friend/coworker Beth. She promised she would. I went on to tell her that I had a vision for what the cover was supposed to look like, but I had no idea how to begin getting a book published. And just like God had promised, he sent me the "how." Beth said her daughter, Marley, had helped someone publish a book this summer and would know just what to do.

Wow. God had gone and wowed me twice that day!

Now, I'm guessing you've read all the way to this point and have a question that you are hoping I'll answer. I bet I know what that question is. It's the same question that was on everyone's mind when they found out Max had a tumor. I know it was on mine. The question is, Does Max have cancer?

On the last night I planned to work on this book, God sent me something to include in order to answer that question. Here goes.

I know that we didn't get the pathology report back until after we left the hospital, which, from what we were told, was a good thing. The longer it takes to get the report back, the less concerning the tumor is and the less likely that the tumor is cancer.

When we got the phone call that the pathology report was back, I asked the oncologist if it was benign. She gave me a vocabulary lesson on what "benign" meant, and basically said it could be a tricky question. She said that by definition, benign means that it doesn't cause the body harm. Well, Max's tumor had caused his body harm. She went on to say that the type of tumor he had was not the kind that would spread to other areas of the body, and that it was not the type that would for sure come back. It was slow growing instead of fast, and that was good.

That's all I got on the phone. I was sort of numb after that conversation. I had no idea whether it was cancer or not. I couldn't come out and ask her, because Max was in the room. I knew he knew what cancer meant. I also knew he didn't know what "benign" meant.

We went to her office the next week to get the results. Bryan, Max, and I showed up expecting to leave either devastated or relieved. That's also the day she told us about Jacksonville being our radiation destination, so we were kind of dumbfounded that day. Leaving the Atlanta area for radiation treatments was not something we had even thought about. Emory in Atlanta has a radiation facility, and we had assumed that was where we would go. So, we were in a state of shock when going to Jacksonville for at least six weeks of radiation was her preferred method to treat Max's tumor area as a preventative for it to never come back. They had proton beam, and Emory did not.

But, she never mentioned cancer. Again, I asked if the tumor was cancerous, and she gave me another vocabulary lesson on what "malignant" and "benign" meant without coming right out and saying it was for sure cancer. She didn't mention it until I asked, and then she gave us a vague answer and said if we wanted to say he had cancer, we could.

Well, I did not want to if I didn't have to! In hindsight,

ironically, I think she was trying to talk in code to me since Max was in the room, and I just wasn't getting it.

Someone else told me that the type of tumor Max had was a gray area. He had the "good" kind of that type of tumor (there are several different grades of that particular tumor), and sometimes they could be cancerous, in that they come back again. I have chosen not to research it on my own. I'm not mentioning the name of the tumor on purpose, because I don't want others to, either.

Maybe the tumor was cancer. Maybe that's why Max had to have radiation. That makes sense, right? You don't get radiation if you don't have cancer, do you? I don't know, because I refuse to research it.

I know we learned about radiation in Max's online science class while in Jacksonville. By definition in the medical field, his online video said radiation could be used to treat cancer. So, maybe that is what we are doing, treating cancer.

But . . . technically, there is no cancer, even if it had been cancerous. On the day of surgery, the neurosurgeon told us that he had gotten 99 percent of the tumor. That meant 1 percent was left. That 1 percent was what we were going to treat with radiation. That night, we sent out an update and prayer request to our prayer warriors for God to take that 1 percent away.

Well, the next day, Max had another MRI—the one that worried me so; the one for which he wasn't sedated. The results from that MRI showed *no residual tumor*. There was 0 percent tumor left. Nothing there!

The MRI that he underwent in Jacksonville a few weeks later showed *no residual tumor*. Nothing there again!

Y'all, God answered so many prayers for us. We needed best-case scenario, a tumor like Jell-O, Max to heal quickly, and have no post-surgery side effects, no baby tumors to be found in the spinal tap, that 1 percent residual tumor to be gone when they did the post-surgery MRI, and no side effects of radiation. Then, we needed his four-month postoperative MRI to be clear . . . *and it was!* God answered each of those prayers. He did. Lots of people prayed, and God answered those prayers. But, the biggest part is we believed He could do it.

And. He. Did.

So, as far as the question of cancer goes, technically, my baby does not have cancer. Maybe he did, maybe he didn't. I honestly don't know or care at this point. That gray area we were told about may be something in the medical world. I don't even know. What I do know is that there are no gray areas with God. You either trust in Him, or you don't. You either surrender everything to Him, or you don't. You either believe Jesus died on the cross for you, or you don't. You either ask God to save you, or you don't. You either go to Heaven, or you don't.

We chose to surrender everything and enter this race to wait on Him to guide us. *But God* knew we would surrender when He set us on this journey, this race. He had been testing our family for a few years. He knew.

Is our race really over? Have we really gotten the checkered flag? Will there be another race with more laps and delays? We don't know, *but God* does. And In God We Trust.

God is good. His mercy endures forever. I will forever be grateful for the grace He has shown us. That grace allowed us to find joy in this race He set before us.

> *O give thanks unto the Lord; for he is good: for his mercy endureth for ever.*
>
> —Psalm 136

About the Author

Lori Grant lives in Dawsonville, Georgia, with her husband, Bryan, and two children, Mattie and Max. They have two dogs, Sparky and Axle. When they aren't at the dirt-bike races, the Grant family loves to travel to places that have bodies of water, and spend family time together every chance they get. They love to go to the family lake house in North Georgia or to the Gulf beaches.

Max's first time behind the pulpit after telling his preacher calling at our 2018 revival. He's holding a card from one of the little girls in our church. She made him the card to let him know she loved him. He used the card in his sermon.

Max's last race with a tumor. He was racing on Saturday, and we found the tumor on Monday. He felt so bad that day, but gave it all he had. He tried to make it through the whole weekend, but just couldn't do it. He usually never wanted to leave early.

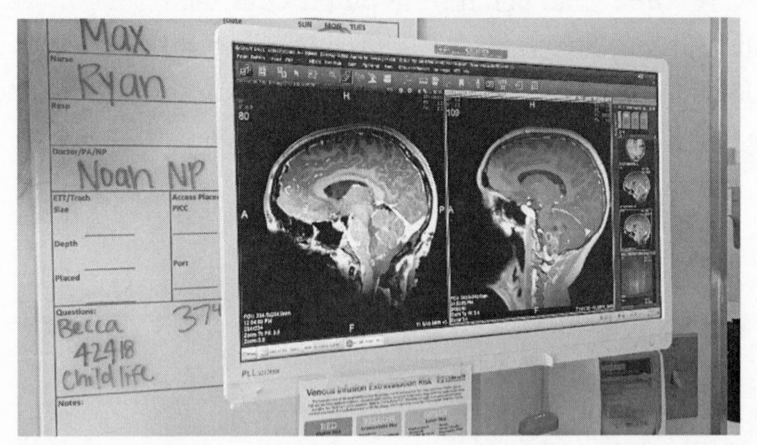

Max's first MRI that shows the tumor between his brain stem and cerebellum.

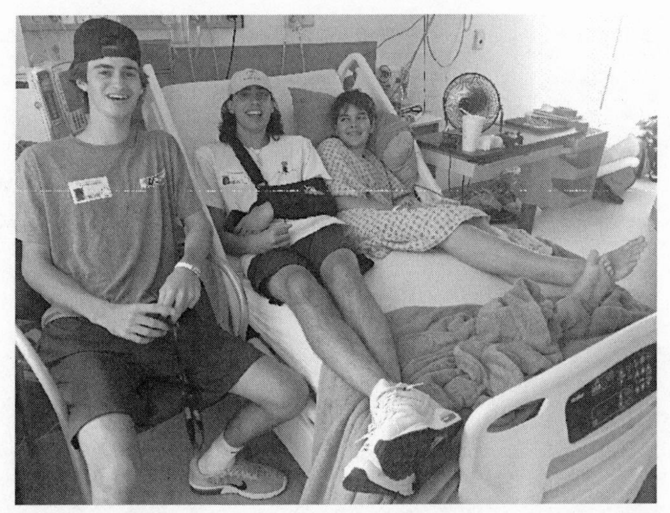

Max's "brothers" came to visit as soon as they could that Tuesday after we found out he had the tumor. Will and Gavin always make him smile!

Just a few of the family and friends who came to visit Max on Wednesday before his surgery on Thursday. He put a brave smile on his face despite his nervousness. Some are racing friends, some are church friends, some are family, but all are like family.

The youth who didn't come to the hospital on Wednesday night met at the church to pray for Max. Prayer works!

Some of the Grant cousins! These sweet ones came to visit and pray with us on Wednesday night, too!

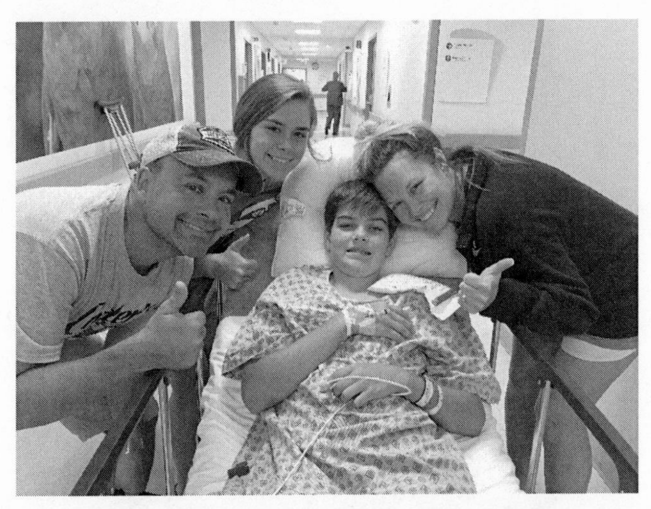

This was as far as they would let us go with Max on surgery morning. The sweet nurse took our picture. We knew #Godhasthis the whole time, so we were able to smile!

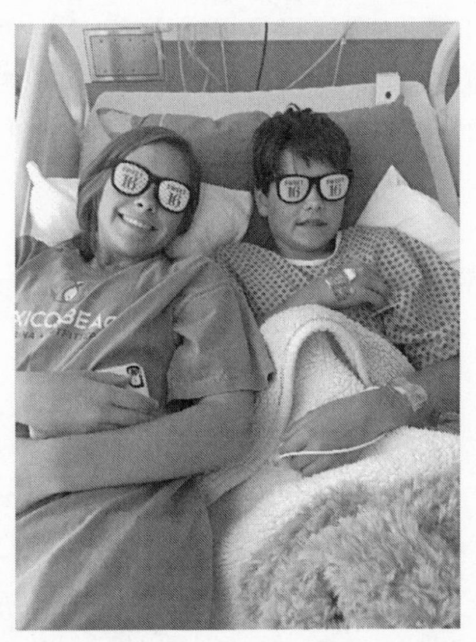

The Sunday after surgery was Mattie's sixteenth birthday. This picture shows where she stayed most of the time when we didn't have visitors: right by his side.

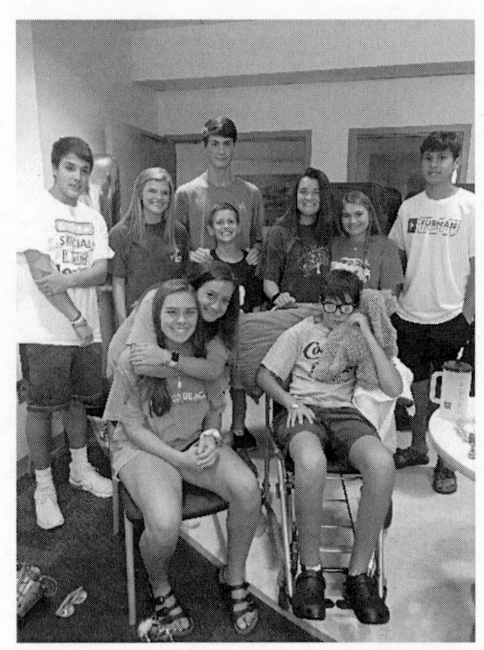

The birthday gang came to celebrate the birthday girl! So what if it was in a waiting room? They still made her feel special, and Max ventured out for a few minutes for the very first time since surgery!

Max ringing the chimes! Best day ever!

Our sweet family came all the way to Jax to see him ring the chimes! He is so loved!

The last time Max ever had to wear the radiation mask was the best day. Notice how it resembles dirt-bike gear!